# Cut Flo

*Prolonging Fr*

*Second Edition*

Grateful acknowledgement is given to the following for the use of photos:

Ball Seed Co., especially Will Healy, Joe Seals and Lisa Segroves; California Protea Management and Marketing for Pink Ice protea; Marc Cathey; Clause for Paxia snapdragon; De Vroomen Holland for Hennie Graafland astilbe; Mike Evans, University of Florida for lilium hybrids; FloraCulture International magazine; Goldsmith Seeds for Knight Mix carnation; GrowerTalks magazine; Monrovia Nursery Company for Blue Skies lilac; Netherlands Flower Bulb Information Center for allium, Orange Wonder dahlia, eremurus, Unsurpassable narcissus and Kees Nelis tulip; Orchids by Hausermann, Inc. for cattleya, cymbidium and dendrobium; PanAmerican Seed Co. for Mona Lisa anemone, Bouquet Mix sweet pea and Pulcino Mix zinnia; Sakata Seed America, Inc. for Heidi Mixed eustoma; Twyford Plant Laboratories, Inc. for Sharonii heliconia; Van Staaveren/Aalsmeer for Little Princess Lilies alstroemeria; Walters Gardens, Inc. for aconitum and paeonia; and Yoder Bros., Inc. for Conquista chrysanthemum.

Cover photo courtesy California Cut Flower Commission.

# Cut Flowers

## *Prolonging Freshness*

### Second Edition

Postproduction Care & Handling

John N. Sacalis

Edited by Joseph L. Seals

Ball Publishing

Batavia, Illinois USA

Ball Publishing
335 N. River Street
P.O. Box 9
Batavia, Illinois 60510 USA

Printed in the United States of America

98 97 96 95 94 93    5 4 3 2

Ohio State University hopes that users of this book will find it useful and
informative. While the author has endeavored to provide accurate
information, Ohio State University asks users to call its attention to any
errors. The author has attempted to obtain information included in this
book from reliable sources; however, the accuracy and completeness of
this book and any opinion based thereon are not guaranteed. No endorse-
ment is intended for products mentioned, nor is criticism meant for
products not mentioned.

Library of Congress Cataloging in Publication Data

Sacalis, John N. 1927-
    Cut flowers : prolonging freshness / John N. Sacalis : edited by
Joseph L. Seals. -- 2nd ed.
        p.  cm.
    Includes bibliographical references and index.

    ISBN 0-9626796-7-4 : $42.00
    1. Cut flowers—Handling    2. Cut flowers—Postharvest technology.
    I. Seals, Joseph L.    II. Title.
     SB442.5.S23    1993                              92-45174
     635.9'666—dc20                                   CIP

# CONTENTS

# FOREWORD

*C* *ut Flowers: Prolonging Freshness* is one of a series of books about the care and handling of plants from grower to consumer. It's designed to give the entire marketing-user chain of grower, wholesaler, retailer and consumer the current recommendations on the most effective procedures for each postproduction stage—as each has its own specific considerations.

While we may think that using fresh flowers for enjoyment and to express emotion is a modern custom, it's actually an ancient tradition dating back at least 50,000 years to some Neanderthal burial caves where, in recent excavations, dried bouquets of flowers have been discovered. These same plants are still found growing in surrounding areas today and have survived virtually unchanged to modern times. We, too, haven't changed that much over the centuries, and fresh cut flowers still express our joys and sorrows and celebrate life's memorable as well as quiet moments.

Because fresh cut flowers symbolize so much, their lasting quality is very important to the receiver and needs to be equally as important to growers. Today, fresh cut flowers have benefited from extensive advances in breeding, culture, chemicals and new storage practices. We can now purchase annuals, biennials, perennials and tropical species, and we have the knowledge to ensure their continued success throughout the year. We hope you will find the successful practice of postproduction care begins here.

The Postproduction series includes the following four books: *Bedding Plants:*

*Prolonging Shelf Performance* by Allan M. Armitage, the University of Georgia; *Cut Flowers: Prolonging Freshness (2nd ed.)* by John N. Sacalis, Rutgers University, and edited by Joseph L. Seals; *Flowering Potted Plants: Prolonging Shelf Performance* by Terril A. Nell, University of Florida; and *Foliage Plants: Prolonging Quality* by Thomas M. Blessington, University of Maryland, and Pamela C. Collins, landscape design and interior plantscaping consultant.

These four postproduction books originated from the series produced through the Kiplinger Chair in Horticulture at The Ohio State University, Columbus, OH. During 1980-1981, I occupied the Kiplinger Chair, which is funded by businesses, foundations and individuals to support research and educational activities for floricultural excellence. Since that time, the Kiplinger Chair has been occupied by Drs. Armitage, Blessington, Nell and Sacalis, all of whom authored the books in this series.

The Chair honors Dr. D.C. Kiplinger, professor of floriculture, for his contributions as a teacher, researcher and extension specialist. Recommendations for the Chair urged expanded research in production and distribution of high quality floral products. Thus, the postproduction books on bedding plants, cut flowers, flowering potted plants and foliage plants were subsequently planned and produced.

Committee members during the creation of the guides were: Stanley F. Backman, Minneapolis, MN; Roger D. Blackwell, Columbus, OH, H. Marc Cathey, Beltsville,

MD; for the Ohio Florists Association: Willard H. Barco, Medina, OH, James F. Bridenbaugh, Kent, OH and August J. Corso, Sandusky, OH; Paul Ecke Jr., Encinitas, CA; Harry K. Tayama, Columbus, OH; and for The Ohio State University: Robert A. Kennedy, Steven M. Still and Luther Waters Jr.

**H. Marc Cathey**
National Chair for Florist
    and Nursery Crops Review
U.S. Department of Agriculture
Washington, DC

# INTRODUCTION

F lowers have been used by humankind for thousands of years for adornment, decoration and as a means of expression. The precise time of the discovery that the life of a flower plucked from a plant could be prolonged by placing its stem in water is not known, but that surely marked the beginnings of this book's subject—postproduction care and handling of cut flowers.

A great deal of research dealing with postproduction care of cut flowers has been carried out in recent years. Our understanding of cut flower physiology, however, is really quite rudimentary, despite the development of techniques that enable us to maintain good cut flower quality longer than ever before.

This book's purpose is to present easy-to-access information on the best techniques for improving the vase life of cut flowers. Although every effort was made to make maximum use of scientific literature, some of the recommendations were gleaned from articles in trade journals from all over the world.

# POSTPRODUCTION FACTORS

Although it seems obvious that the circumstances under which plants are grown can affect the life of their cut flowers, very little hard data actually substantiates this. In general, any condition—nutrition, moisture or light intensity—that promotes the growth of lush, soft tissues may also predispose the harvested flowers to infection by disease organisms and invasion by pests. This has been clearly documented in chrysanthemum and carnation. Temperature during production is an influential factor in some plants.

## Development stage at harvest

The longevity of many cut flower species is related to the stage of development at harvest. Vase life is usually shortened when flowers are harvested at relatively advanced stages of maturity, but there are exceptions to this. Narcissus, for example, appears to do best when harvested open.

Many flowers last longer when cut at very early developmental stages, and a large number of species—including standard chrysanthemums, carnations and lilies—do extremely well if harvested in the bud stage and opened in special opening solutions. Bud cutting has several benefits aside from allowing a longer period before the onset of senescence. Flower buds are less susceptible to damage by gases such as ethylene than are open, mature flowers. In addition, buds require less careful handling than open blooms, which are more easily damaged in transit.

There are varietal differences in the ability of cut buds to open properly. Most iris varieties, for instance, will develop if cut when a small amount of color extends above the sheath. One variety, however, Professor Blaauw, must be harvested at a more advanced stage—when the edge of one of the petals has opened—in order for the bloom to develop properly in an opening solution.

## Food availability for respiration

All living things require a source of food to provide energy for maintenance and development. Cut flowers are no different. While attached to the plant, flowers have a constant source of food in the form of carbohydrates produced by photosynthesis. Once cut, flowers no longer have this food source if they are kept in relatively low light conditions. Cut flowers usually last longer if harvested after a protracted period of photosynthesis. Harvesting flowers in the afternoon, after exposure to light, rather than in the morning when stores of food have been exhausted by darkness, generally lengthens postharvest life.

The best way to be sure that an adequate supply of sugar is available to cut flowers is to add it to the vase water. Added sugar enables buds to develop properly and attain larger sizes, as well as increases overall longevity. Sugar may be dissolved in water at concentrations of 1% to 7% to be fed constantly, or 5% to 12% to be pulsed overnight. Flowers pulsed in this manner are usually held in plain water for the remainder of their lives.

The foliage of some flowers, such as roses, may be burned by excessive sugar uptake. This may be remedied by first hydrating the flowers in a solution without sugar and then placing them in a floral preservative or by using a lower concentration of sugar in the floral preservative.

## Light

Very little research has been done on the effects of light on longevity of cut flowers; it isn't known to significantly affect vase life. We do know, however, that exposing bud cut flowers to light promotes color intensity when they are opened and inhibits yellowing of foliage during storage.

## Temperature

The rate of senescence or aging in flowers held in water is directly proportional to the rate of respiration which, in turn, is dependent on temperature. A high respiration rate leads to rapid carbohydrate depletion. This means that a higher temperature will result in a much shorter vase life for flowers in water. Florists use refrigeration to retard utilization of carbohydrates during respiration and to extend vase life and delay development.

Unopened cartons of flowers generate considerable heat even in cool areas, because the heat created by respiration is not dissipated. Bring flowers to storage temperature as quickly as possible and maintain proper temperatures for maximum vase life.

The addition of carbohydrates to the vase water minimizes the carbohydrate depletion that occurs at higher temperatures.

Certain species, especially tropicals, easily sustain chilling damage. Tempera-tures suitable for many other flowers may ruin more sensitive species. Wherever known, optimum holding temperature recommendations are given for specific crops.

## Irrigation

Whenever possible, cut flowers should be hydrated with water from which salts have been removed—known as deionized water. Water can be deionized by passing it through a column or by using reverse osmosis equipment.

Water that is somewhat acidic (about pH 2.5 to 3.5) is taken up by flower stems much more readily than alkaline water. Since water supplies in many areas contain minerals that make the water very "hard" or alkaline, proper hydration of flowers often presents a problem.

Alkaline water can be acidified by the addition of citric acid or aluminum sulfate. Citric acid is cheaper to use and more effective. The proportion of citric acid varies with the type and amount of the water's mineral content. The best way to determine the correct amount of citric acid needed to bring tap water to a pH of 3.5 is to make a stock solution of citric acid, and add small amounts to the water or preservative solution—checking the pH after each addition—until a pH of 3.5 is attained. It's helpful for future reference to make a note of the total amount of stock solution used. Hard water generally requires from 300 to 500 ppm of citric acid. Hydroxyquinoline citrate (HQC) lowers pH somewhat. If HQC is to be used in the holding solution, include it in the water when establishing the level of citric acid required. Aluminum sulfate is less desirable as an acidifier and may even be phytotoxic at low pH.

If these chemicals are not available, the juice of one lemon in one liter (approximately one quart) of water will usually lower the pH to about 3.0 if the mineral content of the water is relatively low. High alkaline or "hard" water requires a larger quantity of lemon juice. In a pinch, a small amount of lemon juice concentrate will do the job.

Water uptake is also governed by the temperature of the solution. At 100°F (38°C) water is less viscous and is taken up by flowers much more readily than at a temperature of 39°F (4°C).

## Blockage by air in the stem

When stems are cut, air is drawn into them for a short distance forming air plugs or embolisms. These air plugs can prevent the normal movement of water through the stem once it is placed in water. This loss in ability to take up water can be minimized by placing stems in slightly acidified water— pH 3.0 to 4.0—or by recutting stems underwater. Using warm water at about bath temperature—100°F (38°C)—also inhibits the formation of embolisms.

## Physiologic blockage

With very few exceptions, the amount of water taken up by a flower decreases with time. This phenomenon is known as physiologic blockage.

## Physical blockage by microorganisms

The effects of bacteria and fungi can often be seen when foliage is allowed to remain in the vase water to rot, fouling and clouding the solution. Microorganisms thrive and multiply on decaying plant tissue and are taken up into the stem where they form a physical barrier to water uptake. Consequently, the flower wilts and dies.

Since such microorganisms multiply even more rapidly in the presence of sugar, the use of sugar as a food source in the holding solution or vase water results in increased blockage and even more rapid wilting.

Whenever sugar is used, a biocide must be added to prevent the proliferation of microorganisms. The simplest floral preservative contains sugar and a biocide. Other compounds that further enhance flower quality are also present in most preservatives.

The most common biocide is 8-hydroxyquinoline citrate (HQC), which retards microbe growth and is fairly safe to use with most flower species, although it is toxic to some. HQC is slightly acid, which enhances water uptake. The normal concentration of HQC is 200 ppm.

Silver nitrate, applied as a pulse (a 100 to 1,000 ppm stem dip for 10 seconds to 10 minutes) or taken up continuously in the preservative solution (at 25 to 50 ppm) is effective with some flowers. Its use is not generally recommended, however, for several reasons. It is relatively expensive; it can cause blackening; and its effectiveness is reduced by the presence of chlorine, which is found in most tap water. Use silver nitrate only with deionized water.

## Floral preservatives

Numerous commercial preservatives are available to increase the longevity of cut flowers. Most do an excellent job of extending vase life. Be sure to follow directions closely for their use.

For those wishing to make their own preservatives, specific formulations are given for certain species. In addition, several formulations are provided on page 105. It's always best to try out a homemade preservative first on a small scale. In an occasional emergency, lemon or a citrus soda pop containing sugar diluted one-to-one with water makes an acceptable, if somewhat expensive, floral preservative.

There is no single preservative that gives optimum results with all flowers. Cut flowers vary in their requirements, and each species should be treated individually.

## Plant growth regulators

Certain chemicals known as plant growth regulators control growth and/or development. Some of these chemicals are manufactured synthetically, while others, called plant hormones, are made by the plants. There are several plant growth regulators that can affect the aging and longevity of cut flowers.

### Ethylene

Ethylene is an odorless, colorless gas that decreases cut flowers' longevity. It can cause rapid wilting (carnations), shedding or shattering of petals (snapdragons) or other damage to petal tissue (orchids). Ethylene is found in the atmosphere as a product of incomplete combustion. It is also produced by aging plant tissues, such as ripening fruit and senescing flowers.

Flowers vary in their sensitivity to ethylene, but those that are sensitive may be killed by concentrations as low as less than one ppm in less than 12 hours' exposure. To avoid the effects of ethylene, keep flowers away from gas leaks, smoke, ripening fruit and other aging flowers. Holding and work areas should be well ventilated. Sensitivity to ethylene is reduced at lower temperatures, so it is very important to remove flowers from shipping cartons and bring them to their proper holding temperature as quickly as possible. Treatment with silver thiosulfate often eliminates, or at least reduces, the effects of ethylene on many sensitive species of cut flowers.

### Auxin

There are data that indicate that endogenous auxins affect the aging of cut flowers, but little is known of the commercial applications of this information. However, small concentrations of auxin, such as 2,4-D found in some herbicides, can rapidly kill cut flowers. Don't store flowers in containers that have been used for weed killer of any kind.

The tips of certain spiked flowers, such as snapdragons, have a strong tendency to curve upward when held in a horizontal position, even for very short periods. This curvature is caused by gravity and is an auxin-mediated effect. Always store spikes in an upright position to prevent gravitational bending.

### Gibberellins and cytokinins

These growth regulators have been found to affect flower longevity. Gibberellins— gibberellic acid in particular—are useful in promoting bud development and reducing yellowing in stored flower foliage, especially in lilies.

Although cytokinins are reported to increase the vase life of anthurium and daffodils and retard foliage yellowing in other species, they are not used commercially with these crops to any significant extent.

### Abscisic acid

This growth regulator is associated with aging in plants and is related to ethylene production. It has no commercial application to prolong the life of cut flowers.

## Pests and diseases

Injury from pests and diseases during production reduces cut flower quality and longevity.

After harvest, cut flowers are predisposed to infection by Botrytis, or gray mold, particularly if moisture collects on flower tissue surfaces. Unopened cartons of flowers left in the heat and then chilled contain large quantities of condensation, which often results in spoilage by gray mold. Prolonged storage, even at proper temperatures, can lead to the same disease.

## Handling damage

Injury to cut flower tissue from improper handling can decrease vase life by making tissues more susceptible to infection by bacteria and fungi. Affected flowers produce large quantities of ethylene which, in turn, promotes rapid floral senescence.

## Storage

Storage techniques and conditions for optimum vase life vary from one cultivar to the next. Some flowers are pulsed with silver thiosulfate and/or a preservative prior to storage. Some are stored dry, some in water or a preservative solution, while others do equally well stored either wet or dry. For best results, follow specific recommendations for temperature, relative humidity and moisture barrier for each species.

While proper storage will ensure maximum longevity for most cut flowers, prolonged storage can result in decreased vase life. Keep in mind that there are reasonable limits to storage time if flower performance is not to be sacrificed.

## Miscellaneous chemical effects

Fluoride has a detrimental effect on plants in the lily family, causing leaf scorching. Cut flowers in this family are also affected by fluorine, which is found as an additive in most drinking waters. Fluoride is most damaging at low pH, which is best for optimum water uptake. Avoid using water with high fluoride content.

The sap exudate from the base of some species' stems decreases the vase life of other flowers when drawn up into vascular tissues. This is particularly true of Narcissus, which shortens the life of other blooms held in the same container.

## Floral foams

Anchoring cut flower stems has always presented a challenge to floral designers. Open celled floral foams have helped to solve the problem by permitting positive placement of flowers in a material that allows good water uptake and promotes longevity.

Before use, thoroughly soak floral foams by allowing them to float in the solution. Most flowers benefit from the addition of a floral preservative to the soaking solution. Don't try to speed up absorption by holding the foam under the surface. This creates air pockets resulting in poor performance.

When arranging flowers, make sure that stem bases are in contact with the foam. If a flower is inserted too deeply, remove it completely and reinsert it making sure there is no gap between the foam and the base of the stem.

Tests indicate the possible presence of substances in floral foams that may cause a reduction in vase life. Some brands contain higher levels of these substances than others. The effects of these substances may be minimized by soaking foam in a floral preservative instead of plain water. Many excellent brands of floral foams are now being marketed, and it is relatively simple to determine which ones offer the greatest longevity. Set flowers in a vase solution to which a preservative has been added. Then anchor flowers of the same species in foam that has been soaked in the same preservative. Compare the two to see if there is a significant reduction in longevity as a result of using the foam. If there is, test other brands until there is no appreciable difference in vase life. Solutions in containers that are used for soaking foam blocks should be changed frequently to prevent the buildup of substances detrimental to flower longevity.

## Skin sensitivity

Some people suffer skin ailments as a result of handling flowers. A glycosidic substance found in tulips and alstroemeria has been identified as the cause of a dermatitis known as tulip fingers, which can be quite incapacitating.

A skin rash, sporotrichosis, can be contracted from contact with a fungus that thrives in wet floral storage areas. Simple skin afflictions may also be caused by allergic reactions to various substances derived from plant tissues or from contact with pesticide or herbicide residues. Recently, a dermatitis has been associated with harvesting of Queen Anne's lace (*Ammi majus*).

Many problems can be prevented by simply protecting the skin. Dusting hands with talc and wearing surgical gloves, or coating hands with a good sealant, provides a good protective barrier.

# CROPS

# *Acacia* spp.

Includes: *A. baileyana, A. cultriformis, A. dealbata, A. decurrens*
Family Name: **Mimosacenae (formerly Leguminosae)**
Common names: **Wattle, Mimosa**

Shrubs or small trees with clusters of yellow flowers. Native to Australia and the tropics.

ACACIA

## Postproduction factors

**Development at harvest.** Acacia may be harvested at bud stage and forced at retail. It can be sold as "green mimosa" with unopened flowers or "yellow mimosa" with opened flowers.

**Lasting qualities.** Longevity is increased by use of preservative.

**Hydration.** Adjust to pH 3.5 and maintain water temperature of 105° to 115°F (41° to 46°C). Allow to absorb for 8 hours. Note: Never place in metal buckets or vases.

**Temperature.** Mimosa suffers from drastic changes in temperature.

## Retail handling

**Preparation.** Recut stems upon receiving flowers.

**Hydration.** Place stems in clean, warm water—adjusted to pH 3.5—for 2 hours.

**Preservative.** Transfer flowers to a preservative solution.

**Bud opening.** Force bud cut acacia in the dark at 75°F (24°C).

**Storage.** Flowers become desiccated rapidly. Store at 95% to 100% relative humidity. Hold blooms in plastic wrap with stems in a preservative solution. Bud cut acacia may be stored in water up to 25 days at 33°F (0.5°C) after forcing.

## Consumer care

Recut stems as soon as possible. Place flowers in clean, acidified water for 2 hours. (The juice of one lemon added to about 1 quart [.6 l] of vase water will raise water acidity.) Transfer flowers to a vase containing a floral preservative. Place in a cool location, away from rapid air movement. Acacia loses water quickly and has a ten-

# *Acacia* spp.

a-*kay*-shee-a

dency to dry out, so provide as much
humidity as possible.

ADDITIONAL READING

Anon. 1984. Mimosa: extending the cold storage of
flower sprays as required; vase life performance.
*Horticulturae Francaise* 163:19-24.

# *Aconitum napellus*  a-kon-*ee*-tum na-*pel*-lus

Also: *A. carmichaelii, A.* x *bicolor*
Family Name: **Ranunculaceae**
Common Names: **Aconite, Monkshood, Wolfsbane**

Herbaceous, tuberous-rooted perennial. Flowers similar to delphinium—but hooded—in shades of blue, violet or purple with a few white or pink. Poisonous. Native to temperate areas.

ACONITE

## Postproduction factors

**Development at harvest.** Harvest when the first flowers of the cluster have opened.

**Lasting qualities.** Flowers last 12 to 14 days. Also suitable as dried material.
**Preparation.** Strip foliage that would be below water level.
**Preservative.** Silver thiosulfate solutions show positive results.

## Retail handling

**Preservative.** Use a floral preservative to enhance vase life.

## Consumer care

Recut stems as soon as possible, and place flowers in clean water containing a floral preservative. Avoid placing near extremes of heat or cold.

ADDITIONAL READING
Kalkman, F.C. 1982. Pretreatment improves the quality of summer flowers. *Vakblad voor de Bloemisterij* 38:26-29.
Tijssen, G.C.M. 1978. The culture of Aconitum has possibilities. *Vakblad voor de Bloemisterij.* 33:28-30.

# *Allium giganteum*  a-*lee*-um gi-*gan*-tee-um

Also: *A. aflatunense, A. caeruleum, A. sphaerocephalum*
Family Name: **Amaryllidaceae**
Common Names: **Giant Onion, Drumstick Allium**

**Widespread plants from bulbs, some with characteristic onion odor. Flowers in globose heads in white and shades of blue and purple.**

ALLIUM GIGANTEUM

## Postproduction factors

**Development at harvest.** Harvest when at least one-third of the flowers on the umbel have opened.

**Lasting qualities.** Allium can last up to 14 days without storage.

**Preservative.** Allium responds favorably to preservative solutions.

**Storage.** Storage reduces vase life.

## Retail handling

**Preparation.** Recut allium stems immediately upon receipt.

**Preservative.** Place flowers in a preservative solution adjusted to pH 4.0.

**Temperature.** Refrigerate blooms at 40° to 45°F (5° to 7°C).

## Consumer care

Recut allium stems, and place flowers in a vase of clean water containing a floral preservative.

ADDITIONAL READING
Anon. 1979. *Annual Report.* Wageningen, Netherlands: Sprenger Institute.
Bardendse, L.V. 1979. More attention to keeping quality in summer flowers. *Vakblad voor de Bloemisterij* 34:34-35.
Bakker, J. 1979. Which minor bulb crops react favorably to cut flower vase life preservatives? *Bloembollencujltuur* 89:804-805.
Holstead, K.L. 1985. Exotics: handle with care. *Florists' Review* October 10.
Kalkman, E.C. 1984. Storage has a negative influence on the vase life of Allium and Eremerus. *Vakblad voor de Bloemisterij* 39:33.

# *Alstroemeria* hybrids     ahl-strurm-*e*-ree-a

## Family Name: **Alstroemeriaceae**
## Common Name: **Peruvian Lily**

**Tuberous-rooted perennials, native to South America. A complex hybrid involving three or more species. All shades of pink, salmon, orange, red and lavender, most with intricate throat markings.**

DWARF ALSTROEMERIA

## Postproduction factors

**Development at harvest.** Flowers develop best if harvested when color just begins to show. Locally shipped flowers may be harvested up to the time when the first three flowers have opened.

**Lasting qualities.** Alstroemeria lasts approximately 1 week in water and up to 2 weeks in a preservative solution.

**Preservative.** Preservatives with high sugar content may cause foliage yellowing. Some reports show only marginal increase in longevity with preservatives.

**Ethylene.** Alstroemerias are sensitive to ethylene, which induces forced unfolding of buds and shortens vase life.

**Special handling.** Foliage bruises easily. Remove excess foliage and wrap stems in plastic sleeves to minimize damage.

## Retail handling

**Preparation.** Recut stems upon receipt.

**Pretreatment.** Pulse with silver thiosulfate to reduce effects of ethylene exposure.

**Hydration.** Place flowers in a hydrating solution at pH 3.5. Alstroemeria may be damaged by exposure to fluoride; avoid using water with high fluoride content.

**Preservative.** After hydration, transfer flowers to a preservative solution that is not too high in sugar.

**Storage.** Properly treated flowers may be stored up to 1 week at 35°F (2°C).

**Skin sensitivity.** Handling alstroemeria may cause dermatitis. Protect hands.

## Consumer care

Recut stems and place flowers in clean water containing a floral preservative. Be

A

sure to remove all foliage below the solution level. If flowers have been out of water for some time, place in plain water—acidified if possible—for 2 hours. Then transfer to a vase containing a preservative. Do not expose alstroemeria to temperature extremes or rapid air movement. Note: Frequent contact may cause skin rash.

**ADDITIONAL READING**
Anon. 1979. *Annual Report.* Wageningen, Netherlands: Sprenger Institute.

Anon. 1985. Pretreatment dramatically improves flower life. *World Flower Trade Magazine* September.

Heins, R.D. and H.F. Wilkins. 1977. Alstroemeria cultural research, University of Minnesota. *Minnesota State Florists' Bulletin* February.

Molnar, J. 1975. Alstroemeria—a promising new cut flower. *Ohio Florists' Association* Bulletin No. 553.

Reid, M.S. 1986. "Postharvest care and handling of cut flowers." University of California at Davis. April 15, draft version.

Woltering, E.J. and H. Harkema. 1981. Ethylene damage to cut flowers. *Bedrijfsontwikkeling* 12:193-196.

# *Anemone* hybrids

Family Name: **Ranunculaceae**
Common Name: **Poppy Anemone**

**Herbaceous, tuberous-rooted perennials. Popular cut flower. Anemones are hybrids of *A. coronaria* with other species. Cup-shaped flowers come in white and shades of purple, blue, red, pink and bicolors. Native to the north temperate zones.**

MONA LISA MIX

## Postproduction factors

**Development at harvest.** Harvest after allowing the flower to open and close once.

**Lasting qualities.** Vase life is usually 3 to 6 days. Flowers can last as long as 10 days.

**Preservative.** Anemones respond favorably to floral preservatives.

**Ethylene.** Flowers are sensitive to ethylene, which shortens vase life.

**Miscellaneous chemical effects.** Exudate from narcissus stems causes limp stems in anemones.

## Retail handling

**Preparation.** Recut stems upon receipt.

**Hydration.** Hydrate flowers in warm water at pH 3.5 containing silver thiosulfate for 12 to 24 hours.

**Preservative.** Transfer blooms to a preservative solution at 80° to 100°F (27° to 38°C) containing no more than 2% sugar. Loosen bunches to allow flowers to open.

**Ethylene.** Keep anemones away from ethylene sources. Pulse with silver thiosulfate to minimize effects of ethylene exposure.

**Temperature.** Condition and hold flowers at 40°F (5°C).

**Miscellaneous chemical effects.** Don't use anemones in arrangements with daffodils or narcissus.

## Consumer care

Recut stems and place flowers in a dilute preservative solution. Keep anemones away

A

from temperature extremes and rapid air movement. If possible, avoid using with daffodils or narcissus.

---

**ADDITIONAL READING**

Anon. 1980. *Retail Florists' Guide to Care and Handling*. Alexandria, VA: Society of American Florists.

Anon. 1977. Ornamental Plants. *Annual Report*. Wageningen, Netherlands: Sprenger Institute.

Bakker, J. 1979. Which minor bulb crops react favorably to cut flower vase life preservatives? *Bloembollencultuur* 89:804-805.

Barendse, L.V.J. 1974. Damage caused by Narcissus slime to various flower species. *Vakblad voor de Bloemisterij* 29(21):12-13.

Ferrera, L.J. 1985. *Anemone coronaria,* Mona Lisa. *Pennsylvania Flower Growers' Bulletin* 362.

Piskornik, M. 1983. The longevity and water relations of cut poppy anemone flowers (*Anemone coronaria* L.). *Prace Instytutu Sadownictwa i Kwiaciarstwa w Skierniewicach B* 8:191–198.

# *Anthurium* ✕ *cultorum*

an-*thewr*-ree-um
kul-*tor*-um

Family Name: **Araceae**
Common Names: **Anthurium, Flamingo Flower, Hawaiian Heart**

A

Aroid flowers with showy red, purple, pink, white or greenish spathe. Native to tropical Americas. A complex group of hybrids involving primarily *A. andraeanum.* The dark green, heart-shaped leaves are sometimes used in arrangements.

ANTHURIUM

## Production factors

**Disorder.** Spadix rot may develop under high temperature and high humidity conditions.

## Postproduction factors

**Development at harvest.** Maturity is determined by the proportion of open flowers on the spadix. Spadices with open flowers appear rough. Flower development starts at the spadix base and moves upward. Vase life of anthurium harvested at a more mature stage—when three-fourths of the lower portion of the spadix is rough and three-fourths of the flowers are open—is longer than that of flowers harvested at earlier stages. Flowers picked too early wilt quickly.

**Lasting qualities.** Vase life, when flowers are properly handled, ranges from 14 to 28 days. Light flowers with shorter, thinner stems have a longer vase life than heavier flowers with long, thick stems. Senescence is most often the result of water stress. Most of the water lost evaporates from the spadix.

**Ethylene.** Wound-generated ethylene at the stem bases causes nonbacterial clogging of the stems. Application of silver nitrate is more effective than silver thiosulfate. Pretreating anthuriums in 1,000 ppm silver

# *Anthurium* **X** *cultorum*

nitrate for 10 to 60 minutes can increase vase life by more than 50%.

**Plant growth regulators.** Although not widely used, a dip in a cytokinin, such as 10 ppm N-6-Benzyladenine, is reported to increase vase life and reduce susceptibility to chilling injury.

**Temperature.** Anthuriums are temperature sensitive. Exposure to temperatures below 55°F (13°C) can cause chilling injury, indicated by darkening of the spathe.

## Retail handling

**Preparation.** Unpack flowers and recut stems.

**Pretreatment.** Pulse anthuriums in 1,000 ppm silver nitrate solution for 10 to 40 minutes to prevent reduced vase life from excessive evaporation. *Always use deionized water with silver nitrate*. Mist with water and cover with polyethylene film.

**Hydration.** Moisture loss from the spadix may be reduced by dipping the whole flower in a carnauba wax emulsion, such as a 3% solution of FMC Wax 819—or other fruit wax. Place flower stems in water until the wax is dry. This treatment can double the longevity of anthuriums. Also, recut stalks periodically to reduce the possibility of wilting.

**Preservative.** Anthuriums respond favorably to preservative solutions.

**Temperature.** Refrigerate anthuriums at 55°F (13°C). Lower temperatures may cause chilling damage.

## Consumer care

Recut stems and immerse flower *heads* in water at room temperature for 10 minutes if the heart-shaped spathe appears to be wilted. Then place stems in a preservative solution made with clean water. Replace solution every 3 days. Keep flowers away from temperature extremes and strong sunlight.

ADDITIONAL READING

Kalkman, E.C. 1983. *Vakblad voor de Bloemisterij* 38(51/52):69-71.

Paull, R.E., N.J. Chen and J. Deputy. 1985. Physiological changes associated with senescence of cut anthurium flowers. *Journal of the American Society of Horticultural Scientists* 110:156-162.

Paull, R.E. and T.T. Goo. 1985. Ethylene and water stress in the senescence of cut anthurium flowers. *Journal of the American Society of Horticultural Scientists* 110:84-88.

Paull, R.E.. 1983. Extending postharvest life of anthuriums: use of waxes. Research Extension Series. *Hawaii Institute of Tropical Agriculture and Human Resources* No. 037:225-226.

Paull, R.E. and T. Goo. 1982. Pulse treatment with silver nitrate extends vase life of anthuriums. *Journal of the American Society of Horticultural Scientists* 107(5):842-844.

Reid, M.S. 1986. "Postharvest care and handling of cut flowers." University of California at Davis. April 15, draft version.

Staby, G.L., J.L. Robertson, D.C. Kiplinger and C.A. Conover. 1976. Proceedings of national conference on commodity handling. *Horticulture Series* No. 432. Ohio Florists' Association.

Sullivan, G.H., J.L. Robertson and G.L. Staby. 1980. Postharvest care and handling of fresh flowers and greens. *Management for Retail Florists with Applications to Nurseries and Garden Centers*. San Francisco: W.H. Freeman and Company.

# *Antirrhinum majus*  an-tee-*ree*-num *mah*-yus

## Family Name: **Scrophulariaceae**
## Common Name: **Snapdragon**

**Semihardy perennial, treated as an annual. Shades of red, pink, salmon, orange, bronze, yellow, lavender, white and bicolors. Native to the Mediterranean region.**

PAXIA

## Production factors

**Pollination.** Bee pollination of snapdragons causes premature senescence and petal drop, making flowers unsalable. Cover crop with cheesecloth to prevent pollination. Double flowered varieties are more difficult for bees to pollinate.

## Postproduction factors

**Development at harvest.** Snapdragons are usually harvested for local markets when one-half to two-thirds of the flowers on the spikes have opened. Harvest flowers at a less mature stage—when one-third of the flowers have opened—for storage and shipping to distant locations.

**Lasting qualities.** Flowers held in plain water last 5 to 7 days. When treated with silver thiosulfate and placed in a preservative solution, snapdragons can last 10 to 16 days.

**Spike curvature.** Snapdragons are extremely sensitive to gravity. Spikes held for even a short period in a nonvertical position quickly curve upward—sometimes in a matter of minutes—assuming a permanent bend near their tips. This spike curvature significantly reduces flower quality.

**Preservative.** Snapdragons held in a preservative solution have a longer vase life than those held in plain water. However, uptake of sugar causes stretching of spikes and separation of florets, somewhat reducing quality.

**Light.** Flowers in plain water have a

A

reduced vase life when exposed to light levels of 200 fc (2.2 klux) or more. Light does not affect longevity of flowers held in a preservative solution and actually enhances the color of opening buds. When snapdragons are held in plain water and opened in darkness, their color—particularly in red and pink cultivars—tends to be faded.

**Water.** Cut snapdragons appear to be tolerant of widely varying water qualities. As much as 1,000 ppm soluble salts in the holding solution does not adversely affect longevity. Similarly, fluoride levels must be as much as 3 ppm before flowers are injured.

**Temperature.** Snapdragons freeze at 30°F (-1°C).

**Ethylene.** Snapdragons—especially older varieties—are sensitive to ethylene, which causes rapid petal drop. Some of the newer cultivars have been selected for resistance to ethylene; however, a high concentration of ethylene will cause damage to any of the varieties.

## Retail handling

**Special handling.** Store snapdragons in a vertical position to prevent spike curvature.

**Preparation.** Recut snapdragon stems.

**Hydration.** Hydrate flowers in clean, warm—100° to 110°F (38° to 43°C)—water adjusted to pH 3.5.

**Pretreatment.** Immerse stems in an STS solution containing 0.1 ounce concentrate per gallon plus 2% sucrose and 300 ppm 8-hydroxyquinoline citrate for 24 to 72 hours to improve vase life and flower quality.

Allow a 2-hour uptake of 30 ppm N-1-naphthylphthalamate to reduce response to gravity and resulting spike curvature.

Treat snapdragons with silver thiosulfate to reduce the effects of ethylene. Pulse flowers at room temperature—70°F (21°C)—in a silver thiosulfate solution at the recommended rate. Snapdragons may benefit by including 7% sucrose in this solution. *Flowers that have been previously treated with silver thiosulfate should not be retreated at retail.*

**Preservative.** Transfer bud-cut flowers to a preservative solution. To reduce spike stretching caused by sugar in the preservative, add 10 to 25 ppm of n-dimethyl-amino succinamic acid (Alar, B-Nine) to the solution.

**Light.** If flowers are held in plain water, keep in darkness.

**Temperature.** Refrigerate snapdragons at 32° to 33°F (0° to 1°C).

**Storage.** Store snapdragons in a vertical position—dry or in water—at 40°F (5°C) for no more than 3 to 4 days. To increase longevity to 7 to 10 days, wrap spikes in plastic film and place in water. Snapdragons have been successfully stored for 3 weeks, but long-term storage often yields poor bud development and faded color.

## Consumer care

Recut stems and remove foliage that will be below the water line. Place flowers in a preservative solution in a cool location. Avoid heat and drafts. Don't place snapdragons near ripening fruit.

# *Antirrhinum majus*    an-tee-*ree*-num  *mah*-yus

**ADDITIONAL READING**

Anon. 1980. *Retail Florists' Concise Guide to Care and Handling*. Alexandria, VA: Society of American Florists.

Anon. 1986. Florist cut flower care guide. *Florist March,* 19(10).

Apelbaum, A., and M. Katchansky. 1977. Improving quality and prolonging vase life of bud cut flowers by pretreatment with thiabendazole. *Journal of the American Society of Horticultural Scientists* 102(5):623-625.

Nowak, J. 1981. Chemical pretreatment of snapdragon spikes to increase cut flower longevity. *Scientia Horticulturae* 15(3):255-262.

Reid, M.S. 1986. "Postharvest care and handling of cut flowers." University of California at Davis. April 15, draft version.

Staby, G.L., J.L. Robertson, D.C. Kiplinger and C.A. Conover. 1976. Proceedings of national conference on commodity handling. *Horticulture Series* No. 432. Ohio Florists' Association.

Sullivan, G.H., J.L. Robertson and G.L. Staby. 1980. Postharvest care and handling of fresh flowers and greens. *Management of Retail Florists with Applications to Nurseries and Garden Centers*. San Francisco: W.H. Freeman and Company.

Yee, S.W., J.K. Suh and S.M. Roh. 1980. The effect of cold, dry storage and preservative solution treatment on the vase life of snapdragon (*Antirrhinum majus*) cut flowers. *Journal of the Korean Society of Horticultural Scientists* 21(3):193-197.

A

# *Argyranthemum frutescens* ar-gi-*ran*-the-mum froo-*tes*-enz

## Family Name: **Asteraceae (formerly Compositae)**
## Common Names: **Marguerite Daisy, Paris Daisy**

**Formerly classified as *Chrysanthemum frutescens*. White or yellow single composites with branched stems. Flowers are often tinted various pastel colors.**

MARGUERITE DAISY

## Postproduction factors

**Development at harvest.** Harvest when most blooms on the branching cluster have fully opened.

**Lasting qualities.** Flowers last 3 to 8 days. A number of buds may develop during vase life. Storage reduces vase life.

**Pretreatment.** Pulse overnight in 25 ppm silver nitrate and 0.5% sugar. (More than 0.5% sugar can cause yellowing of leaves.)

**Problems.** Flowers are injured by even low concentrations of the germicide 8-hydroxyquinoline citrate.

**Storage.** Marguerites may be stored dry—in hampers—up to 3 days at 39°F (4°C). Longer storage reduces vase life. Insufficient cooling or excessive heat in daisy hampers may cause yellowing of foliage or development of disease in marguerites.

## Retail handling

**Preparation.** Remove marguerites from daisy hampers as soon as possible. Open bunches and recut stems. Remove as much of lower foliage as possible.

**Hydration.** Hydrate overnight in a warm solution—100°F (38°C)—adjusted to pH 3.5 with citric acid. Use the same solution for holding flowers under refrigeration. Don't use 8-hydroxyquinoline citrate (HQC).

**Temperature.** Refrigerate marguerites at 32° to 40°F (0° to 5°C).

## Consumer care

Recut stems and remove lower leaves. Place flowers in a vase of fresh water. Add a floral preservative to vase water to encourage bud opening.

**ADDITIONAL READING**

Byrne, T.G. and D.S. Farnham. 1980. Postharvest treatments for marguerite daisies. *Florists' Review* March 27.

Kofranek, A.M., H.C. Kohl and J. Kubota. 1975. Stabilized chlorine compound as a vase water additive. *Flower and Nursery Report* January/February.

Koths, J.S., A. Botacchi and J. Maisano. 1986. *Chrysanthemum frutescens*. Connecticut Greenhouse Newsletter, 131. January.

Reid, M.S. 1986. "Postharvest care and handling of cut flowers." University of California at Davis. April 15, draft version.

A

# Astilbe X arendsii     a-*stil*-bee  ah-*rendz*-ee-ee

## Family Name: **Saxifragaceae**
## Common Names: **Astilbe, Perennial Spirea**

**Perennials grown for their showy panicles or plumes of small white, rose or pink flowers.**

HENNIE GRAAFLAND

## Postproduction factors

**Development at harvest.** Pick when nearly all flowers on the panicle are open. Buds on flowers cut when the plumes are half open don't develop further in water and develop only slightly in a preservative solution.

**Lasting qualities.** Flowers last 5 to 8 days if kept in water. Leaves tend to drop off before flowers.

**Ethylene.** Astilbe flowers are sensitive to ethylene.

## Retail handling

**Pretreatment.** Treat astilbe with silver thiosulfate to prevent damage from exposure to ethylene.

**Hydration.** Hydrate astilbe in warm, slightly acidified water.

**Temperature.** Keep flowers at 35° to 40°F (2° to 5°C).

## Consumer care

Recut stems and place flowers in a warm preservative solution. Avoid high temperatures and rapid air movement. Keep flowers away from ripening fruit.

ADDITIONAL READING

Kalkman, E.C. 1984. Correct stage of cutting astilbe is important for vase life. *Vakblad voor de Bloemisterij* 39(12):28.

Krogt, T.M. van. 1984. Four astilbe cultivars suitable as cut flowers. *Vakblad voor de Bloemisterij* 39(12):29-31.

Woltering, E.J. 1984. Ethylene susceptibility of summer flowers. Pretreatment prevents damage. *Vakblad voor de Bloemisterij* 39(17):34-37.

# *Bouvardia* hybrids

boo-*var*-dee-a

Family Name: **Rubiaceae**
Common Name: **Bouvardia**

B

**Large shrubs with fragrant, single or double tubular, white, pink or scarlet flowers in cymes. Native to Central and South America.**

BOUVARDIA

## Postproduction factors

**Development at harvest.** Harvest when one or two flowers in the bunch have opened. Harvest white flowered forms when fully colored but unopened.

**Lasting qualities.** Bouvardia held in a preservative solution generally last 1 week, but can last as long as 2 to 3 weeks. Bouvardia flowers last longer if all foliage and shoots developing outside the umbel of flowers are removed.

**Temperature.** Do not allow holding temperature to drop below 50°F (10°C).

**Disorders.** Some bouvardia flowers are cut at the umbel base and shipped in small, closed boxes covered with plastic film and sealed to prevent moisture loss. Flowers packaged in this manner have a tendency to become infected with gray mold, or *Botrytis cinerea*. Treat boxes with a fungicide to discourage Botrytis.

## Retail handling

**Preparation.** Recut stems and remove all foliage and shoots.

**Hydration.** Hydrate bouvardia in clean, warm water—adjusted to pH 3.5 with citric acid—for 2 hours.

**Preservative.** Transfer flowers to a preservative solution for optimum vase life.

**Temperature.** Refrigerate bouvardia at temperatures *no lower than 45°F (7°C)*.

## Consumer care

Remove excess foliage, recut stems and place flowers in clean, warm water containing a preservative. Avoid conditions that promote moisture loss, such as high temperatures, low humidity and rapid air movement. Recut stems frequently.

# *Bouvardia* hybrids

boo-*var*-dee-a

**ADDITIONAL READING**

Anon. 1986. Dutch bouvardia plentiful. *Canadian Florist* August, 81(8):33.

Glas, R. 1984. Bouvardia grown just as well under double glass. *Vakblad voor de Bloemisterij* 39(20):37.

Papenhagen, A. 1983. Bouvardia. *Lehr- und Versuchsanstaltfur Gartenbau.* Friesdorf, German Federated Republic 83(4):72-76.

Tompkins, C.M. 1950. Botrytis blight of bouvardia flowers. *Hilgardia* 19:399-408.

Zeller, C.C. 1986. Home is where the care continues. *Florist* March, 19(10).

B

# *Callistephus chinensis*

**Family Name: Asteraceae (formerly Compositae)**
**Common Name: China Aster, Chinese Aster**

**C**

Annuals with a variety of ray floret colors. Native to Asia. Several strains offer a wide variety of flower forms.

MILADY SERIES

## Production factors

**Disorders.** China asters suffer from aster wilt, a fungus, and aster yellows, a viruslike disease. Both can be fatal or can disfigure stems and flowers, impeding water uptake.

## Postproduction factors

**Development at harvest.** Harvest when flower is partially to wide open.

**Lasting qualities.** Flowers generally last 5 to 7 days, but can last up to 15 days.

**Preservative.** Flowers held in a preservative solution have a longer vase life. Pulse China asters for 10 seconds with a highly concentrated (1,000 ppm) silver nitrate solution to increase vase life by 5 days.

**Problems.** Tissue below the solution level has a tendency to decay and develop a foul odor. Flowers in bacteria-laden solution wilt and die of water stress. Use a bactericide to prevent premature decay.

**Storage.** Store flowers pretreated with silver nitrate for up to 1 week at 35°F (2°C).

## Retail handling

**Control of bacteria.** The following methods are suggested to control bacteria:

(1) Before hydration, dip stems in 1,000 ppm silver nitrate for 10 minutes. Flowers treated with silver nitrate last two to three times as long as untreated flowers. Do not recut stems.

(2) Add 8-hydroxyquinoline citrate to retard bacterial buildup.

**Hydration.** Use clean water adjusted to pH 3.5 with citric acid.

**Temperature.** Keep flowers at 35° to 40°F (2° to 5°C).

# *Callistephus chinensis*

## Consumer care

Recut stems, remove excess foliage, and place flowers in a preservative solution.

ADDITIONAL READING

De Nijs, L.P. 1981. A study on the keeping quality of some summer annuals. *Verbondsnieuws voor de Belgische Sierteelt* 25(13):609-611.

Kofranek, A.M., E. Evans, J. Kubota and D.S. Farnham. 1979. Chemical pretreatment of China aster to increase flower longevity. *Flower and Nursery Report.* Spring.

Kofranek, A.M., H.C. Kohl and J. Kubota. 1975. Stabilized chlorine compound as a vase water additive. *Flower and Nursery Report.* January-February.

——. 1974. New vase water additive better than sucrose alone. *The Grower* August 17.

Marousky, F.J. 1977. Control of bacteria in cut flower vase water. *Proceedings of the Florida State Horticultural Society.* Published 1978. 90:294-296.

Reid, M.S. 1986. "Postharvest care and handling of cut flowers." University of California at Davis. April 15, draft version.

C

# *Cattleya* hybrids　　　　　*kat*-lee-a

## Family Name: **Orchidaceae**
## Common Name: **Orchid**

**Large, showy epiphytic orchids, many of which are characteristically orchid or purple in color. Also occurs in shades of white, yellow and orange or combinations of these colors with purple. At one time, the most popular of the florists' orchids and still the traditional corsage orchid. Actually a group of complex hybrids including this genus and *Laelia, Brassavola* and *Sophronitas*— all usually sold as cattleya. Native to tropical Americas.**

CATTLEYA HYBRID

### Production factors

**Disorders.** Orchids are susceptible to viral diseases. For this reason, propagation by tissue culture has become popular. Pollination causes premature senescence.

### Postproduction factors

**Development at harvest.** Orchids are normally harvested when flowers are open. Bud cut flowers usually fail to develop.

Individual flowers or spikes with several flowers are harvested and shipped with stems in vials containing solution. Vials are taped to the bottoms of cardboard cartons, with the flowers supported by shredded waxed paper to prevent bruising.

**Lasting qualities.** Corsage life is from 4 to 5 days if kept cool.

**Ethylene.** Orchids are very sensitive to ethylene. In addition to usual sources, pollination causes production of ethylene that results in premature senescence. Levels of ethylene as low as 2 parts per billion can cause dry sepal injury, characterized by progressive drying and bleaching of sepals. Silver thiosulfate treatment does not appear to improve longevity.

**Temperature.** Refrigeration at lower than 60°F (15°C) may cause chilling injury in some cultivars, evidenced by browning of the throat (column and labellum) and a water soaked appearance in petals and sepals.

**Storage.** Orchids are not normally stored for very long. Flowers may be kept for approximately 1 week at normal refrigeration temperatures.

## Retail handling

**Hydration.** Make sure vials are filled with solution.

**Ethylene.** Protect orchids from even minute sources of ethylene. Do not use silver thiosulfate.

**Temperature.** Refrigerate orchids at 55° to 60°F (13° to 15°C). Lower temperatures may cause chilling injury.

## Consumer care

If orchids are in a corsage, don't refrigerate below 50°F (10°C). Place in a plastic bag with a piece of moist paper. If orchids are received as cut flowers in water, recut stems and place in a preservative. Keep orchids away from ripening fruit.

ADDITIONAL READING

Anon. 1980. *Retail Florist's Concise Guide to Care and Handling.* Alexandria, VA: Society of American Florists.

Anon. 1986. Florist cut flower care guide. *Florist* March. 19(10).

Davidson, O.W. 1949. Effects of ethylene on orchid flowers. Proceedings of the American Society of Horticultural Scientists 53:440-446.

Goh, C.J., A.H. Halevy, R. Engel and A.M. Kofranek. 1985. Ethylene evolution and sensitivity in cut orchid flowers. *Scientia Horticulturae* 26(1):57-67.

Reid, M.S. 1986. "Postharvest care and handling of cut flowers." University of California at Davis. April 15, draft version.

Staby, G.L., J.L. Robertson, D.C. Kiplinger and C.A. Conover, 1976. Proceedings of national conference on commodity handling. *Horticulture Series* No. 432. Ohio Florists' Association.

Sullivan, G.H., J.L. Robertson and G.L. Staby. Postharvest care and handling of fresh flowers and greens. *Management for Retail Florists with Applications to Nurseries and Garden Centers.* San Francisco, CA:W.H. Freeman and Company.

Zimmer, K. 1980. Lasting quality of orchid cut flowers. *Deutscher Gartenbau* 34(8):343-344.

C

# *Cymbidium* hybrids

sim-*bid*-ee-um

## Family Name: **Orchidaceae**
## Common Name: **Cymbidium**

**Spray orchids occurring in white and shades of pink, rose, yellow and green with rose or pink lip. Native to tropical parts of Malaysia and Asia.**

CYMBIDIUM

## Postproduction factors

**Lasting qualities.** Cymbidiums easily last 2 weeks in solution and are widely used as corsage flowers. The lowest flowers on an inflorescence generally have the shortest longevity. Flowers left intact on the inflorescence keep longer than detached flowers.

**Preservatives.** Use a preservative to increase vase life and reduce bending of inflorescences.

**Ethylene.** Cymbidiums are affected by ethylene but are less sensitive than cattleya. Exposure to ethylene causes discoloration of flowers. Silver thiosulfate (an inhibitor of ethylene action) and oxyamino acetic acid (an inhibitor of ethylene synthesis) partially inhibit ethylene production in emasculated flowers but appear to stimulate it in pollinated flowers. Both chemicals decrease coloration by inhibiting anthocyanin synthesis in the column.

**Temperature.** Refrigerate cymbidiums at 50° to 55°F (10° to 13°C) for maximum longevity.

**Shipping.** Insert stems of whole sprays or individual flowers in vials containing a holding solution and tape (or otherwise attach) to bottoms of cardboard cartons to prevent shifting. Protect blooms by packing with shredded waxed paper.

## Retail handling

**Preparation.** Recut the bases of inflorescences with multiple flowers.

**Preservative.** Place stems in fresh preservative and check vials periodically to make sure they contain sufficient solution. Wrap stem bases of corsage flowers in moist cotton.

**Ethylene.** Avoid exposure to ethylene.

**Temperature.** Hold at 50° to 55°F (10° to 13°C) for longest life.

# *Cymbidium* hybrids

sim-*bid*-ee-um

C

## Consumer care

Recut stem bases of spray cymbidiums and place in a floral solution. Place corsage flowers in a plastic bag with a piece of moist paper. Keep cymbidiums away from smoke, ripening fruit and wilting flowers. Avoid extremes of heat and cold.

ADDITIONAL READING

Anon. 1980. *Retail Florist's Concise Guide to Care and Handling.* Alexandria, VA: Society of American Florists.

Barendse, L.V. 1978. The keeping quality of cymbidiums. *Vakblad voor de Bloemisterij* 33(13):20-21.

Goh, C.J., A.H. Halevy, R. Engel and A.M. Kofranek. 1985. Ethylene evolution and sensitivity in cut orchid flowers. *Scientia Horticulturae* 26:57-67.

Harkema, H. and E.J. Woltering. 1981. Ethylene damage to cut flowers and forced shrubs. *Vakblad voor de Bloemisterij* 36(22):40-42.

# *D*ahlia hybrids

dah-lee-a

Family Name: **Asteraceae (formerly Compositae)**
Common Name: **Dahlia**

**Hybrids originated from parents. All colors except blue. Enormous variation in flower form. Native to mountains of Guatemala and Mexico.**

ORANGE WONDER

## Postproduction factors

**Development at harvest.** Harvest only when the flower is fully opened; unopened blooms wilt readily.

**Lasting qualities.** Vase life is about 1 to 2 weeks when a floral preservative is used. Pretreatment increases longevity.

**Preservative.** Longevity is somewhat longer when glucose rather than sucrose is used in the preservative formulation.

**Ethylene.** Dahlias are moderately sensitive to ethylene; 1 ppm can affect flower quality. Pretreatment reduces damage and extends normal vase life.

**Pretreatment.** Use either a pulse or continuous uptake of 10% glucose and 0.2 mm silver nitrate added to the holding solution for maximum vase life.

**Special handling.** It is common practice for growers to scald the lower few centimeters of dahlia stems before shipping to allow continued water uptake.

## Retail handling

**Pretreatment.** Pulse dahlias in a floral preservative containing 10% glucose and 25 mg per liter silver nitrate (0.17 ounces per 5 gallons) to assure maximum vase life and reduce shattering of petals from ethylene exposure.

**Hydration.** After pulsing, transfer flowers to clean water. Use a good quality water adjusted to pH 3.5 to 4.0 with citric acid for hydration.

**Temperature.** Keep flowers at 35° to 40°F (2° to 5°C).

# *Dahlia* hybrids

*dah*-lee-a

## Consumer care

Recut stems and sear ends a moment in a flame, or scald one-half inch (1.3 cm) of stem base in boiling water. Place flowers in clean, warm preservative solution. Keep dahlias out of direct sunlight and away from rapid air movement. Avoid high temperatures as well. Flowers may shatter prematurely if kept near ripening fruit.

**ADDITIONAL READING**

Lukaszewska, A.J. 1983. The effect of continuous and 24 hour sugar feeding on carbohydrates and free amino acids in the inflorescences of cut dahlias. *Prace Instytutu Sadownictwa i Kwiaciarstwa w Skierniewicach B*. 8:207-214.

——. 1983. The effect of continuous and 24 hour sugar feeding on the keeping quality of cut dahlias. *Prace Instytutu Sadownictwa i Kwiaciarstwa w Skierniewicach B. (Rosliny Ozdobne)* 8:199-205.

Staden, O.L. 1976. Preservatives for extending the life of cut flowers are particularly valuable. *Vakblad voor de Bloemisterij* 31(34):44-45.

Woltering, E.J. 1984. Ethylene susceptibility of summer flowers. Pretreatment prevents damage. *Vakblad voor de Bloemisterij* 39(17):34-37.

D

# *Delphinium* hybrids

del-*fin*-ee-um

**D**

Family Name: **Ranunculaceae**
Common Name: **Delphinium**

**Hybrids from parents. Native to the north temperate zones. Includes three distinct groups of hybrids: *D.* x *belladonna, D.* x *cultorum* (most commonly grown) and newer university (and similar) hybrids. Flowers range from blue or violet to rose and occur on spikes.**

PRINCESS CAROLINE

**Lasting qualities.** Properly treated stems can last up to 14 days.

**Ethylene.** Flowers are highly sensitive when exposed to ethylene at 3 ppm for 24 hours at 70°F (21°C). Silver thiosulfate treatment reduces damage and improves vase life of delphiniums exposed to exogenous ethylene.

## Retail handling

**Pretreatment.** Pulse with silver thiosulfate to minimize ethylene damage and prolong vase life.

**Hydration.** Hydrate delphinium in clean, warm water at pH 3.5 to 4.0.

**Preservative.** Use a floral preservative for maximum longevity.

**Temperature.** Refrigerate delphiniums at 35° to 40°F (2° to 5°C).

## Postproduction factors

**Development at harvest.** Harvest when the majority of the flowers on the stem have opened.

## Consumer care

Recut stems and place flowers in clean warm water containing a floral preservative. Avoid temperature extremes. Keep delphiniums away from rapid air movement and ripening fruit.

# *Delphinium* hybrids

ADDITIONAL READING

Loeser, H. 1982. Summer flowers for cutting grown in an unheated plastic house. *Deutscher Gartenbau* 36(45):1878-1881.

Woltering, E.J. 1984. Ethylene susceptibility of summer flowers. Pretreatment prevents damage. *Vakblad voor de Bloemisterij* 39(17):34-37.

# *Dendranthema grandiflora*

den-*dran*-the-ma grand-i-*flo*-ra

Family Name: **Asteraceae (formerly Compositae)**
Common Names: **Florists' Chrysanthemum, Mum, Pompon**

**Formerly classified as *Chrysanthemum morifolium*. Perennial consisting of numerous forms. A hybrid possibly of Chinese origin. All colors except blue.**

D

CONQUISTA

## Production factors

**Fertilization.** Heavy nitrogen application resulting in foliar nitrogen levels of 3.5% and higher can reduce postharvest longevity and increase susceptibility to postharvest Botrytis. Fertilize plants as usual during the first two-thirds of the growing season. Reduce or eliminate nitrogen during the last third of the growing season in order to attain a final N:K ratio of 1:2. Avoid the use of ammonia type nitrogen during winter months or other extended periods of low light to maintain postharvest longevity. It is reported that vase life is best if one-half standard nutrient levels are applied.

**Light.** Partially shade flowers just after they start to show color.

**Temperature.** Chilling temperatures during floral development can reduce quality by causing reddish or pink color to develop in light colored petals.

## Postproduction factors

**Development at harvest.** Pompons are usually harvested when the majority of flowers are open, although bud cut flowers can be developed in opening solutions. Standard mums, however, are harvested either when the flowers are open to a diameter of 2 to $2\frac{1}{2}$ inches (5.1 to 6.4 cm) or when they are still in the bud stage.

**Lasting qualities.** Standard mums last 7 to 14 days, depending on the cultivar. Pompons last 7 days. Foliage usually deteriorates before flowers.

**Light.** Vase life may be increased by holding flowers under lights at approximately 100 fc (1.1 klux) to maintain the

# Dendranthema grandiflora

level of chlorophyll pigment in the leaves.

**Hydration.** Water movement through the woody, basal portion of stems is difficult. Use a good quality, warm water—adjusted to pH 3.5—that contains a bactericide. High HQC levels, however, may cause excessive stem discoloration.

**Preservatives.** Mums respond well to preservatives. Continuous use increases the height of flowers, while use during only the first 3 to 7 days after harvest may result in blooms with flat heads. Sugar levels above 3% may cause yellowing of foliage, particularly in bud cut flowers.

**Plant growth regulators.** Add growth regulator 6-benzyl adenine to the vase solution to inhibit premature leaf yellowing.

**Temperature.** Refrigerate hydrated mums at 32° to 40°F (0° to 5°C).

**Storage.** Store bud cut standard mums that are about 5 inches (13 cm) across dry at 32° to 35°F (0° to 2°C) for up to 3 weeks. Buds 3½ inches (9 cm) across may be stored for 2 weeks, but storage of less mature buds is not recommended. Bud cut mums may also be stored in holding solutions that don't contain sugar.

## Retail handling

**Preparation.** Recut stems, removing basal woody portions. Crushing or pounding stems does not appreciably improve water uptake.

**Hydration.** Freshly harvested, open standard mums: Place freshly cut stems in good quality, warm—100°F (38°C)—water that is low in salts with 25 ppm silver nitrate. Or dip stems for 10 seconds to 10 minutes in 1,000 ppm silver nitrate and then transfer to plain water. Sugar may cause foliage to yellow. Don't use hot water treatments.

*Stored or shipped, open standard mums:* Remove lower foliage along with basal, woody portions when recutting stems. Place flowers in warm water at 100°F (38°C) containing 0.05% Tween 20 and sufficient citric acid to obtain pH 3.5. Place in a cool location, and let stand long enough for flowers to become turgid—about 2 hours. Then transfer to a solution containing 5 to 10 ppm commercial bleach. Do not use sugar.

*Bud cut standard mums:* If time allows, hydrate mums for a short time before placing in an opening solution. To hydrate, use warm—100°F (38°C)—water containing 0.05% Tween 20 and adjusted to pH 3.5 with citric acid. Allow flowers to take up solution in a cool location for about 2 hours—or until they are turgid. Transfer blooms to an opening solution containing no more than 3% sugar and a germicide, such as 25 ppm silver nitrate or 150 ppm 8-hydroxyquinoline citrate. An alternative opening solution that also improves longevity consists of warm—100°F (38°C) —clean water containing 300 ppm 8-hydroxyquinoline citrate and 3% sucrose.

**Light.** Exposure to 50 to 100 fc (.5 to 1.1 klux) of light is beneficial during holding.

**Temperature.** Refrigerate mums and pompons at 30° to 35°F (-1° to 2°C).

## Consumer care

Recut stems and place flowers in a clean container of fresh, warm water. A floral preservative may cause foliage to yellow but will result in longer lasting flowers.

# *Dendranthema grandiflora*   den-*dran*-the-ma grand-i-*flo*-ra

**ADDITIONAL READING**

Apelbaum, A. and M. Katchansky. 1977. Improving quality and prolonging vase life of bud cut flowers by pretreatment with thiabendazole. *Journal of the American Society of Horticultural Scientists* 102(5):623-625.

Bredmose, N. 1982. Tests on the effect of preservatives and of crushing or boiling stems on vase life of cut chrysanthemum. *Meddelelse, Statens Planteavlsforsog* 85(1744):3.

Harkema, H. 1979. Hot water treatment of chrysanthemums by the grower is not advisable. *Vakblad voor de Bloemisterij* 34(38):37.

Ishida, A., M. Masui, A. Nukaya and H. Shigeoka. 1981. Effect of concentrations of nutrient solution on the growth and cut flower life of chrysanthemums. *Journal of the Japanese Society of Horticultural Scientists* 50(1):86-91.

Kofranek, A.M., H.C. Kohl and J. Kubota. 1974. New vase water additive better than sucrose alone. *Grower* 82(7):282.

Kofranek, A.M. and J.L. Paul. 1975. The value of impregnating cut stems with high concentrations of silver nitrate. *Acta Hort* 41:199-206.

Reid, M.S. 1986. "Postharvest care and handling of cut flowers." University of California at Davis. April 15, draft version.

Sullivan, G.H., J.L. Robertson and G.L. Staby. 1980. Postharvest care and handling of fresh flowers and greens. *Management for Retail Florists with Applications to Nurseries and Garden Centers*. San Francisco: W.H. Freeman and Company.

D

# *Dendrobium* spp.

den-*droh*-bee-um

Family Name: **Orchidaceae**
Common Name: **Dendrobium**

Mostly *D. phalaenopsis* cultivars. Spray orchids with canelike pseudo-bulbs. Native to warm and higher parts of American tropical regions.

DENDROBIUM

## Postproduction factors

**Development at harvest.** Harvest dendrobium spikes when most flowers have opened and only the top flowers are in bud.

**Lasting qualities.** Dendrobium vase life is up to 14 days in water, more in preservative. Longevity may vary with the season.

**Preservatives.** Floral preservatives appear to prolong vase life, but preliminary tests have not been confirmed.

**Special handling.** The practice of immersing the bases of cut spikes in boiling water does not significantly improve vase life compared to flowers in a preservative solution, but it does enhance water uptake somewhat. Submerge flowers in water for 10 to 15 minutes for rapid hydration.

**Temperature.** Hold dendrobiums at 50° to 55°F (10° to 13°C).

## Retail handling

**Preparation.** Recut dendrobium stems.
**Hydration.** Refill vials with preservative solution, and check periodically.
**Temperature.** Hold dendrobiums at 50° to 55°F (10° to 13°C).

## Consumer care

Recut dendrobium stems as soon as possible. Place flowers in fresh water containing a floral preservative. If blooms are in vials, check to make sure there is plenty of solution available to stems. Avoid temperature extremes and areas of rapid air movement. Keep flowers away from ripening fruit.

# *Dendrobium* spp.

den-*droh*-bee-um

**ADDITIONAL READING**

Anon. 1986. Florist cut flower care guide. *Florist* March, 19(10).

Goh, C.J., A.H. Halevy, R. Engel and A.M. Kofranek. 1985. Ethylene evolution and sensitivity in cut orchid flowers. *Scientia Horticulturae* 26(1):57-67.

Kunisaki, J.T. 1976. Dendrobium spikes with floral preservatives. *University of Hawaii Cooperative Extension Service Miscellaneous Publication* No. 134.

Nolte, F. 1985. Longevity of cut dendrobium for Thailand. *Deutscher Gartenbau* 39(45):2178.

D

# *Dianthus caryophyllus*

die-*an*-thus
ka-ree-oh-*fil*-lus

**Family Name: Caryophyllaceae**
**Common Name: Carnation**

**Widely used in the florist industry. Many colors. Some originate from the Mediterranean region; others come from Siberia, Arctic America, Japan and the Himalayas.**

KNIGHT MIX

## Production factors

**Nutrient level.** The source of nitrogen during winter months greatly affects vase life. Ammonium nitrate or sodium nitrate produces flowers with a longer vase life than does ammonium sulfate or urea. Extremely low levels of calcium or potassium produces flowers with decreased vase life, but moderate nutrient deficiencies do not greatly affect longevity.When cut flowers are held in 8-hydroxyquinoline citrate, the source of nitrogen during production is not significant.

**Light.** Carnation flowers from plants grown at relatively high light intensity generally have a longer postharvest life than flowers grown at lower light levels.

**Temperature.** Plants grown at 75°F (24°C) have larger flowers with stronger stems than flowers grown at 60°F (15°C). Vase life, however, is shorter.

## Postproduction factors

**Development at harvest.** Carnations may be harvested open or in the bud stage. Bud cut flowers are easier to handle and sustain less damage in packing and shipping. Buds are best harvested for storage when petals have emerged one-fourth to one-half inch (0.5 to 1 cm) above the calyx, but they may open more rapidly when harvested at a slightly more mature stage. Lasting qualities are slightly better for bud harvested flowers, but a disadvantage of bud cuts is uneven opening—or even failure to open.

**Lasting qualities.** Carnations last 6 to 9 days in untreated water, 12 to 16 days in a preservative. Pulsed with silver thiosulfate and held in a floral solution, they last as long as 30 days.

**Preservative.** The vase life of cut carnations is dramatically enhanced by uptake of a preservative solution containing sugar and a germicide. Sucrose is more effective than glucose as a sugar source. Flowers may be pulsed with a high concentration of preservative or provided with a continuous uptake of a lower concentration. Preservatives containing large amounts of aluminum may damage flowers.

**Light.** Exposure of bud cut flowers to about 100 fc (1 klux) yields slightly larger flowers.

**Hydration.** Proper hydration is essential for optimum vase life. Deionized water, with a conductivity of 0.5 to 0.75 mMOHS, is preferable to tap water. Use warm water, 100° to 110°F (38° to 43°C), low in salts and adjusted to pH 3.5 with citric acid. When turgor is restored (2 to 12 hours), transfer flowers to a floral preservative solution.

**Salts.** The following salts in the holding solution improve vase life of carnations: $Ca(NO_3)_2$, $NH_4NO_3$, KCl and $K_2SO_4$.

**Ethylene.** Carnations are sensitive to ethylene at concentrations below 1 ppm, and affected flowers wilt rapidly. Treatment with silver thiosulfate inhibits the effects of ethylene, particularly if given directly following harvest. Flowers pretreated with silver thiosulfate should not be retreated. Flowers at 65°F (18°C) are 1,000 times more susceptible to ethylene damage than flowers at 35°F (2°C), unless they have been treated with silver thiosulfate. Untreated carnation buds are less susceptible to ethylene injury than are open flowers.

**Bacteria.** It is reported that metabolites of several bacteria found in vase water cause extensive blockage of xylem-conducting tissues, resulting in reduced longevity.

**Temperature.** Longevity is increased at lower temperatures—33° to 43°F (1° to 7°C). Exposure to 95°F (35°C) for 3 to 4 hours can drastically reduce vase life. Vacuum cooling techniques to rapidly reduce carton temperatures are promising for carnations shipped long distances and stored.

**Storage.** Select only the best quality flowers for storage. Store carnations dry in polyethylene- or newspaper-lined cartons. Cool rapidly to 32°F (0°C)—optimum storage temperature—and keep at 90% relative humidity. Reduced oxygen levels are not beneficial. Botrytis can be a problem with stored flowers. Bud cut carnations may be stored for up to 4 to 5 weeks, while open flowers may be stored for 2 to 4. Carnations are typically stored for 2 weeks, with no reduction in vase life.

Hypobaric storage of cut carnations has been tried successfully, but this technique is costly and not commonly used. Pulsing carnations with 20% sucrose for 24 hours at 75°F (25°C) allows flowers to withstand a storage temperature of 22°F (-6°C) for 5 days, but untreated flowers cannot tolerate this temperature.

**Shipping.** Carnations are often shipped long distances for extended periods of time. Shipping containers exposed to high temperatures—even a short time in the sun on a loading dock, for instance—can drastically reduce longevity or even prevent buds from developing. Stress caused by shipping results in an accumulation of abscisic acid in floral tissue and renders flowers less responsive to bud opening techniques.

D

# Dianthus caryophyllus

die-*an*-thus
ka-ree-oh-*fil*-lus

## Retail handling

**Preparation.** Unpack flowers as soon as possible. Don't allow unopened cartons to remain in warm areas for extended periods. Don't line up flower heads by inverting stems and bouncing heads on a flat surface. Recut stems cleanly—don't smash them.

**Pretreatment.** Carnations previously treated with silver thiosulfate should not be retreated. Place untreated flowers in a warm solution, adjusted with citric acid to pH 3 to 3.5, containing 1 millimolar silver thiosulfate and 10% sucrose. Hold flowers at 35° to 40°F (2° to 5°C) overnight. Or pulse for 1 to 2 hours at room temperature. Although not quite as effective, an alternative to silver thiosulfate is a 5-minute pulse in 1,000 ppm silver nitrate, then transfer carnations to a floral preservative containing 2% to 4% sucrose.

**Preservative.** After pretreating open flowers with silver thiosulfate, transfer carnations to a preservative solution containing about 2% sugar and a germicide. An alternative solution consists of 3% sucrose and 50 ppm silver nitrate.

**Temperature.** Refrigerate and hold flowers at 40°F (5°C).

**Bud opening.** After pretreating with silver thiosulfate and sucrose (when used), transfer carnation buds to a solution containing 7% sucrose and a germicide. Hold in 100 to 150 fc (1 to 2 klux) of light intensity and 50 to 70% relative humidity.

## Consumer care

Recut stems and remove foliage below the solution level. Place flowers in clean water containing a floral preservative. Avoid temperature extremes.

ADDITIONAL READING

Anon. 1980. *Retail Florists' Concise Guide to Care and Handling.* Alexandria, VA: Society of American Florists.

Cho, H.K. and J.M. Lee. 1979. Studies on extending the life of cut flowers of rose and carnation with various chemical preservatives. *Journal of the Korean Society of Horticultural Scientists* 20:106-110.

Nichols, R., A.M. Kofranek, and J. Kubota. 1982. Effect of delayed silver thiosulfate pulse treatments on carnation cut flower life. *HortScience* 17:600-601.

Reid, M.S. 1986. "Postharvest care and handling of cut flowers." University of California at Davis. April 15, draft version.

———, J.L. Paul, M.B. Farhoomand, A.M. Kofranek and G.L. Staby. 1980. Pulse treatments with silver thiosulfate complex extend the vase life of cut carnations. *Journal of the American Society of Horticultural Scientists* 105:25-27.

Staby, G.L., M.S. Cunningham, C.L. Holstead, J.W. Kelly, P.S. Konjoian, B.A. Eisenberg and B.S. Dressler. 1984. Storage of rose and carnation flowers. *Journal of the American Society of Horticultural Scientists* 109:193-197.

Sullivan, G.H., J.L.Robertson and G.L. Staby. 1980. Postharvest care and handling of fresh flowers and greens. *Management for Retail Florists with Applications to Nurseries and Garden Centers.* San Francisco: W.H. Freeman and Company.

Veen, H. 1979. Effects of silver on ethylene synthesis and action in cut carnations. *Planta* 145:467-470.

D

# *Eremurus* hybrids

e-ray-*meu*-rus

Family Name: **Liliaceae**
Common Names: **Desert Candle, Foxtail Lily**

Tuberous-rooted perennials with tall spikes of tiny, lilylike flowers. Long-lasting flowers in dense racemes that open progressively from the bottom upward. Shades of orange, yellow, cream, pink and white. Native to Asia.

E

*EREMURUS BUNGEI*

## Postproduction factors

**Development at harvest.** Eremurus appears to last best when cut in the bud stage—or when up to one-fourth of the blooms on the spike are open—and then is promptly pulsed in a preservative containing 20% sugar and a biocide. At 70°F (21°C), however, longevity is not markedly affected by the stage of development at harvest.

**Lasting quality.** Flowers last 10 to 18 days.

**Preservative.** Longevity is increased by uptake of a preservative containing sugar and 8-hydroxyquinoline citrate. A 24-hour pulse in a preservative containing 20% sugar and a germicide, as recommended for bud cut flowers above, is a good alternative.

**Ethylene.** Although vase life is only slightly decreased by exposure to ethylene, flowers are damaged and quality is affected by 3 ppm over 24 hours.

**Pretreatment.** Pulse eremurus with silver thiosulfate after harvest for 18 to 20 hours at 45°F (6°C) to prevent ethylene damage.

**Storage.** Vase life decreases with time in storage.

## Retail handling

**Preparation.** Recut eremurus stems.

**Pretreatment.** Pulse flowers in silver thiosulfate overnight in refrigerator.

**Hydration.** Place stems in clean, warm water adjusted to pH 3.5.

**Preservative.** After hydration, transfer flowers to a preservative solution. As an alternative to constant preservative uptake, recut stems upon receipt and place in a preservative containing a germicide and 20% sugar. Store in cooler overnight and then transfer to water.

# *Eremurus* hybrids

**Temperature.** Store spikes up to 3 days at 35° to 40°F (2° to 5°C). Temperatures below 35°F (2°C) may halt flower opening.

## Consumer care

Recut stems and place flowers in a clean container of fresh, warm water to which a floral preservative has been added. Recut stems periodically. Avoid placing flowers near ripening fruit, heat or direct sunlight.

**ADDITIONAL READING**

Bakker, J. 1979. Which minor bulb crops react favorably to cut flower vase life preservatives? *Bloembollencultuur* 89(31):804-805.

Barendse, L.V.J. 1979. More attention to keeping quality in summer flowers. *Vakblad voor de Bloemisterij* 34(20):34-35.

Barendse, L.V.J. 1980. Little is still known about the keeping quality of summer flowers. *Vakblad voor de Bloemisterij* 35(23):40-41.

Holstead, K.L. 1985. Exotics: handle with care. *Florists' Review* October 10:16-19.

Kalkman, E.C. 1984. Storage has a negative influence on the vase life of allium and eremurus. *Vakblad voor de Bloemisterij* 39(28):33.

Krebs, O. and K. Zimmer. 1977. Eremurus as cut flower species. *Deutscher Gartenbau* 31(38):1534-1535.

Woltering, E.J. 1984. Ethylene susceptibility of summer flowers. Pretreatment prevents damage. *Vakblad voor de Bloemisterij* 39(17):34-37.

Zimmer, K. and O. Krebs. 1977. Experiments on propagation, culture and vase life of eremurus. *Deutscher Gartenbau* 31(15):596-601.

E

# *Eustoma grandiflorum*

Also: ***Lisianthus russellianum***
Family Name: **Gentianaceae**
Common Names: **Lisianthus, Sweet Lissies**

Herbaceous biennial plants with bell-like flowers 1½ to 2 inches (4 to 5 cm) across in shades of lavender, purple, pink and white, with some bicolors. Native to North America.

**E**

HEIDI MIXED

## Postproduction factors

**Development at harvest.** Harvest when the first flower on the stalk has opened and a few of the remaining buds are showing color.

**Lasting quality.** The first flower will last up to 1 week; the balance on the stem will open over a period of 1 to 2 weeks.

**Preservative.** Use a preservative to enhance flower color and increase fresh weight and longevity.

## Retail handling

**Preservative.** Use a good floral preservative to improve overall flower quality.

**Storage.** Lisianthus can be held at 35° to 40°F (2° to 5°C) for 2 to 3 days with or without water.

## Consumer care

Recut stems and place flowers in warm water containing a floral preservative. Keep away from direct sunlight and excessive heat.

ADDITIONAL READING
Kalkman, E.C. 1985. Harvest summer flowers when sufficiently mature. *Vakblad voor de Bloemisterij* 40(43):116-117.
Marousky, F.J., T. Sheehan and B. Tjia. 1985. Postharvest petal color of bud cut lisianthus. *HortScience* 20(3):562.

# *Forsythia* X *intermedia*

for-*sith*-ee-a
in-ter-*med*-ee-a

Family Name: **Oleaceae**
Common Names: **Forsythia, Golden Bells**

**Popular yellow-flowered shrub used for forcing buds on cut branches in late winter and early spring. Native to China, Japan and southeast Europe.**

FORSYTHIA

## Postproduction factors

**Development at harvest.** Harvest when buds show color. Forsythias for forcing are generally harvested in late fall in pre-dormant bud stage, stored at 32° to 34°F (0° to 1°C) in a moist, dark atmosphere and forced to bloom as needed at 40°F (5°C).

**Lasting qualities.** With proper care forsythia vase life is up to 3 weeks.

**Preservative.** Use a floral preservative to extend forsythia vase life.

## Retail handling

**Preparation.** Recut a few inches from stem bases with a sharp knife or pruning shears. Don't break or smash stems as this may reduce water uptake capacity.

**Hydration.** Place stems in clean, warm water adjusted to pH 3.5 with citric acid.

**Preservative.** Add a floral preservative to vase water to improve keeping quality.

**Temperature.** Hold branches at 40° to 50°F (5° to 10°C).

## Consumer care

Recut a few inches from bottom of stems with a knife or pruning shears. Don't break stems. Place branches in warm, clean water containing a floral preservative.

ADDITIONAL READING
Anon. 1984. Increased demand for flowering shrub branches. *Holland Flower* December, No. 13.

F

# *Freesia* hybrids

*free*-zhee-uh

Family Name: **Iridaceae**
Common Name: **Freesia**

**Plants propagated from corms or seed with white, yellow, lavender or purple flowers. Most are about 1 to 1½ feet (30 to 45 cm) in height. Original species native to tropical South Africa.**

F

PRESTO MIX

## Production factors

**Disorders.** Viruses are a problem in plants propagated by corms. Make every effort to obtain corms that are certified virus free.

**Miscellaneous chemical reactions.** Plants are sensitive to fluoride, which is normally soluble in acid conditions. Raise soil pH to reduce fluoride availability.

## Postproduction factors

**Development at harvest.** Harvest freesias when the first flower on the inflorescence shows color and is opening, but before the second flower starts to open.

**Lasting qualities.** With proper care, freesias can last 7 to 14 days.

**Problems.** Flowers bruise easily, so handle with care.

**Preservative.** Add a floral preservative to vase water to increase longevity.

**Ethylene.** Freesias are sensitive to ethylene.

**Storage.** Store freesias in water at 35°F (2°C) and about 90% relative humidity for about 1 week.

**Miscellaneous chemical effects.** Freesias are very sensitive to fluoride. A low fluoride concentration—1 ppm—causes browning of leaf tips and prevents maturation of less developed flowers. Vase life is shortened by exposure to exudate from narcissus stems.

## Retail handling

**Preparation.** Recut freesia stems.

# *Freesia* hybrids *free*-zhee-uh

**Pretreatment.** If flowers have not already been pretreated with silver, place stems in warm water containing silver thiosulfate for 2 hours. Then transfer to a holding solution.

**Hydration.** Use tepid water adjusted to pH 3.5 with citric acid to hydrate freesias. Deionized water is best, but good quality tap water is acceptable. Avoid fluoridated drinking water as it may damage both foliage and flowers. Preservatives containing aluminum reduce, but do not completely prevent, symptoms caused by fluoride.

**Preservative.** Use a floral preservative in the holding solution. Tight buds will not develop properly in plain water. Reports indicate that vase life and flower diameter are increased when freesias are placed in a solution containing 4% sucrose, 0.015% aluminum sulfate, 0.2% magnesium sulfate, 0.1% potassium sulfate and 0.05% hydrazine sulfate. An excellent alternative to continuous preservative uptake is pulsing with 2 pounds of sucrose per gallon (10 kg per 4 l) of solution. Allow 18 hours for uptake in the dark at about 70°F (20°C).

**Temperature.** Refrigerate freesias at 35° to 40°F (2° to 5°C).

**Miscellaneous chemical effects.** To assure maximum vase life, do not arrange in the same container with narcissus.

## Consumer care

Recut stems as soon as possible and place flowers in warm, preferably deionized, water to which a floral preservative has been added. Keep freesias away from ripening fruit, and do not place in the same container with narcissus.

ADDITIONAL READING

Anon. 1986. Florist cut flower care guide. *Florist* 19(10), March.

DeHertogh, A. and G. Springer. 1977. Care and handling of spring bulb flowers and plants, Part 1; Suggestions on the use and marketing of bulb flowers and plants, Part 2. *Holland Flower Bulb Technical Services.* Hillegom, Holland: Netherlands Flower Bulb Institute.

Harkema, H. and E.J. Woltelring. 1981. Ethylene damage to cut flowers and forced shrubs. *Vakblad voor de Bloemisterij* 36(22):40-42.

Porterfield, F. 1984. Holland's guide to care and handling. *Florists' Review* August 23, 175(4525):16-17.

Reid, M.S. 1986. "Postharvest care and handling of cut flowers." University of California at Davis. April 15, draft version.

# *Gerbera* hybrids

**Family Name: Asteraceae (formerly Compositae)**
**Common Names: Gerbera, Transvaal Daisy**

Perennial that produces flowers that are very uniform in color and shape. Large, daisy-shaped flowers with petals ranging from white to red, orange and magenta with white or black centers. Previously produced from seedlings that resulted in wide variation in color and form, gerberas are now propagated by tissue culture. Original species native to South Africa and Asia.

G

GERBERA

## Postproduction factors

**Development at harvest.** Most gerberas are harvested when two rows of outer disc florets are open and before pollen shows. When harvested at this time there is usually very little differentiation of conductive and supportive stem tissue about 4 inches (10 cm) below the flower head. Lack of developed supportive tissue in this area may cause stem folding or breaking early in vase life. Some varieties harvested when pollen is showing have less tendency to fold or break.

**Lasting qualities.** Gerberas last 3 to 14 days, depending upon cultivar and conditions. Longevity may be increased significantly by giving a 10-minute pulse of either 1,000 ppm silver nitrate or 1% commercial bleach (sodium hypochlorite) at a ratio of one part bleach to 99 parts water. The 600 ppm sodium hypochlorite solution (1% commercial bleach) plus 0.1% Tween 20 (a surfactant) is often given immediately after harvest to help prevent bacterial blockage. Sucrose at 6% is sometimes added to the bleach pulse. Adding sugar to either of these solutions will further increase vase life but will result in appreciable stem elongation.

**Hydration.** Flowers are harvested by pulling stems from the plant, which leaves a heel at the stem base. Water uptake is impeded if the heel is left intact during hydration.

**Ethylene.** Although gerberas are said to be sensitive to ethylene, exposure to as

**Cut Flowers** *Gerbera*

much as 3 ppm ethylene causes little flower damage; however, vase life may be affected. Ethylene does stimulate growth of the stamen's innermost whorl.

**Plant growth regulators.** A 2-minute immersion of flower heads in 0.1 millimolar Benzyladenine (a cytokinin) is reported to delay the decrease in flowers' fresh weight.

**Temperature.** Gerberas hold up longest when given a cooling period immediately after harvest. A few hours at 35°F (2°C) will remove excess heat. Avoid temperature extremes and low relative humidity.

**Storage.** Cut gerberas may be stored for about 5 days with little or no loss of vase life, but longevity suffers if flowers are stored longer than 1 week. Store in a preservative solution rather than dry or in plain water. Flowers stored dry with heel intact do not take up water well when heel is removed later for hydration. If flowers must be stored dry, remove heel prior to storage.

**Miscellaneous chemical effects.** Flowers are sensitive to fluoride at low concentrations. Symptoms show as brown spotting. If possible, avoid fluoridated water.

## Retail handling

**Hydration.** Use good quality, clean water. Placing flowers in previously used water, even though it may appear to be clean, will shorten vase life. To prevent permanent bending of limp stems that are low in water content, leave gerberas suspended by their heads in perforated cardboard shipping trays during hydration. This allows stems to take up solution without stress until they are turgid. A chicken wire frame may be constructed to suspend

flowers during hydration, but stem injury may result from the wire. For maximum water uptake, hydrate gerberas for 1 to 2 hours in a solution at an initial temperature of 110°F (43°C), adjusted to a pH of 3.5 with citric acid.

**Preservative.** Transfer flowers as soon as possible to a preservative solution containing 25 ppm silver nitrate. A 24-hour delay in preservative application shortens vase life.

**Problems.** Some cultivars wilt prematurely. The exact cause varies from one variety to another. Early wilting may be due to anatomic characteristics, vascular blockage caused by bacteria or some physiologic means.

In addition, many gerbera varieties have a tendency to fold over or break 4 to 6 inches (10 to 15 cm) below the head during early vase life. Little is known about the exact cause or which cultivars are susceptible to stem break, but those exhibiting this problem should be avoided. A 10-minute pulse in 1,000 ppm silver nitrate may avert premature wilting and folding. Greater longevity is obtained with silver nitrate than with silver thiosulfate, which indicates that bacterial contamination, and not ethylene, is the primary problem.

The sodium hypochlorite treatment recommended in *Postproduction factors* also reduces the tendency of gerberas to wilt or fold over. A single recutting of stems reduces both treatments' effectiveness against bacterial plugging. If stems are recut, add 25 ppm silver nitrate to the holding solution. Successive recutting of stems every few days, however, does appear to diminish bacterial plugging. Gerbera stems may elongate as a result of sugar uptake. If elongation is a problem, eliminate sugar and

G

use either the bleach or silver nitrate treatment to increase longevity.

**Temperature.** Hold flowers at 40°F (5°C) the first 3 days to increase vase life. Store gerberas at 35°F (2°C).

**Floral foam.** It is reported that gerberas draw water from floral foams better if stems are inserted and then pulled out slightly, creating a reservoir at the stem tip. No research, however, substantiates this technique.

## Consumer care

Place gerberas in a clean container filled with a warm preservative solution made with clean, preferably deionized, water. If stems have been recut, add 1% commercial bleach to the solution. Avoid temperature extremes; 70°F (21°C) is ideal. Avoid areas of rapid air movement and low relative humidity.

**ADDITIONAL READING**

Dubuc-Lebreaux, M.A. 1985. Histology of the flower stem in *Gerbera jamesoni*. Acta Botanica Neerlandica 34:171-182.

Krader, H.A. and M.N. Rogers. 1983. Effects of pulsing and holding solutions on keeping quality of *Gerbera jamesoni*. *HortScience* 18:614.

Leeuwen, P. van. 1982. Low night temperature has no effect on the lasting quality of gerberas. *Vakblad voor de Bloemisterij* 37:73.

Marousky, F.J. and B. Tjia. 1984. Postharvest occlusion in xylem of cut gerbera peduncle. *HortScience* 19:567.

Reid, M.S. 1986. "Postharvest care and handling of cut flowers." University of California at Davis. April 15, draft version.

Staby, G.L., J.L. Robertson, D.C. Kiplinger and C.A. Conover. 1976. Proceedings of national conference on commodity handling. *Horticulture Series* No. 432, p. 40. Ohio Florists' Association.

Van Meeteren, U. 1978. Water relations and keeping quality of cut gerbera flowers. I. The cause of stem break. *Scientia Horticulturae* 8:65-74.

Woltering, E.J. and H. Haarkema. 1981. Ethylene damage to cut flowers. *Bedrijfsontwikkeling* 12:193-196.

G

# *Gladiolus* hybrids

gla-dee-*oh*-lus

## Family Name: **Iridaceae**
## Common Names: **Gladiolus, Sword Lily**

**Corm-propagated plants with flowers of numerous colors produced on spikes. Original species native to the Mediterranean region and South Africa; the Cape of South Africa is a particularly rich source.**

GLADIOLUS

### Production factors

**Spike curvature.** Plants in a nonvertical position grow upward, resulting in curved spikes of lower quality. This tendency is more pronounced at higher growing temperatures.

**Disorders.** Calcium deficiency during production can result in a disorder known as topple, the breaking over of spikes as they develop.

**Miscellaneous chemical effects.** Plants are susceptible to fluoride injury.

### Postproduction factors

**Development at harvest.** For short distance shipping, gladioli are harvested when a few of the florets are showing color. Spikes are harvested with all buds less developed if long distance shipping is required.

**Lasting qualities.** There are significant variations in the lasting qualities of different gladioli cultivars. Make a note of longer lasting varieties, and purchase gladioli by varietal name.

**Spike curvature.** Tips of spikes are very susceptible to bending due to gravity, especially at higher temperatures.

**Preservative.** The use of preservatives improves bud opening, floret size and vase life. Generally, the earlier the preservative is used, the longer the vase life. Tight buds require preservatives for opening.

**Hydration.** For best results, hydrate gladioli in warm, clean, *deionized* water, adjusted to pH 3.5

**Temperature.** Open bud cut gladioli at 70° to 75°F (21° to 24°C). Temperatures lower than 36° to 41°F (2° to 5°C) may cause chilling injury and prevent flower opening.

**Packing.** Gladioli are usually packed in hampers that are stacked in an upright position so that spikes remain vertical. Precooled flowers are generally packed in regular flower cartons that should remain at low storage temperatures until they are unpacked.

**Storage.** Store gladioli at 35° to 40°F (2° to 5°C) for a maximum of 6 to 8 days. Storage life is reduced to 4 to 6 days at 40° to 50°F (5° to 10°C) and as little as 2 to 4 days at 50° to 80°F (10° to 26°C).

Botrytis can be a problem during storage. Maintain as high a relative humidity as possible without promoting Botrytis growth. Vent storage hampers, and avoid wrapping flowers in moisture-proof material.

**Miscellaneous chemical effects.** *Always use deionized water*. Fluoride, either in the atmosphere or in the holding solution, in concentrations as low as 0.25 ppm (a level common in fluoridated drinking water) is phytotoxic to gladioli. Colored cultivars appear to be more sensitive. Use of a preservative does not overcome the effects of fluoride.

## Retail handling

**Special handling.** Remove the top few buds from spikes to reduce spike curvature and to promote floret opening.

**Pretreatment.** Pulse gladioli 1 hour in a solution of 1,000 ppm silver nitrate followed by a 24-hour pulse in 20% sucrose at 70°F (20°C). Or pulse in a solution containing 20% sucrose, 50 ppm silver nitrate, 300 ppm aluminum sulfate and 250 ppm 8-hydroxyquinoline citrate at air and solution

temperatures of 70°F (20°C) for 20 hours.

**Hydration.** Recut stems and use warm, deionized water adjusted to pH 3.5 for hydration. Tap water may contain sufficient fluoride levels to degrade flower quality. If flowers have been pretreated with silver nitrate, do not recut stems.

**Preservative.** Floral preservatives are very effective in increasing longevity of gladioli. Either add a preservative to the hydrating solution, or transfer hydrated flowers to a preservative solution. As an alternative to commercial preservatives, place stems in a warm holding solution containing 10% sucrose and 300 ppm 8-hydroxyquinoline citrate for 24 to 72 hours at 70°F (20°C). Then transfer to water. This treatment facilitates opening, improves quality and prolongs vase life.

**Temperature.** Refrigerate hydrated gladioli at 35° to 40°F (2° to 5°C).

**Storage.** Pretreated gladioli may be wrapped in paper, placed in cartons and stored at 35°F (2°C) for 10 days. Do not recut stems when flowers are removed from cartons or rehydrated.

## Consumer care

Recut stems and place flowers in clean, warm water containing a floral preservative. Deionized water is recommended but not necessary. Remove a few buds from the spike tips for more uniform opening of florets.

---

**ADDITIONAL READING**
Anon. 1986. Florist cut flower care guide. *Florist* March 19(10).

G

# *Gladiolus* hybrids

gla-dee-*oh*-lus

Anon. 1980. *Retail Florist's Concise Guide to Care and Handling.* Alexandria, VA: Society of American Florists.

Apelbaum, A. and M. Katchansky. 1977. Improving quality and prolonging vase life of bud cut flowers by pretreatment with thiabendazole. *Journal of the American Society of Horticultural Scientists* 102:623-625.

Farnham, D.S., T.G. Byrne, F.J. Marousky, D. Durkin, R. Rij, J.F. Thompson and A.M. Kofranek. 1979. Comparison of conditioning, precooling, transit method and use of a floral preservative on cut flower life. *Journal of the American Society of Horticultural Scientists* 104(4):483-490.

Kofranek, A.M. and J.L. Paul. 1975. The value of impregnating cut stems with high concentrations of silver nitrate. *Acta Hort* 41:199-206.

Kofranek, A.M. and A.H. Halevy. 1976. Sucrose pulsing of gladiolus stems before storage to increase spike quality. *HortScience* 11:572-573.

Reid, M.S. 1986. "Postharvest care and handling of cut flowers." University of California at Davis. April 15, draft version.

Teas, H.J. and T.J. Sheehan. 1959. Control of geotropic bending in snapdragon and gladiolus inflorescences. *Florida State Horticultural Society* 72:437-442.

G

# *Gloriosa rothschildiana*

glo-ree-*oh*-sa
roths-chield-ee-*ah*-na

Also: *G. superba*
Family Name: **Liliaceae**
Common Names: **Gloriosa Lily, Rothschild Lily, Glory Lily**

**Climbing, tuberous-rooted plants with brilliant golden-orange and red flowers. Leaves with long tendril at apex. Native to tropical Asia and Africa.**

GLORIOSA

## Postproduction factors

**Development at harvest.** Harvest when fully open. Gloriosa may be sold on leafless flower stems or on longer main stems with foliage.

**Lasting qualities.** Properly treated flowers last 7 to 10 days.

**Preservative.** Use a preservative to increase longevity.

**Hydration.** Use clean, warm water.

**Storage.** To store dry, pulse flowers in a preservative solution a few hours, bag dry and refrigerate at 35°F (2°C) immediately. Gloriosa may be stored for 3 to 4 days.

## Retail handling

**Preparation.** Recut gloriosa stems.

**Hydration.** Place flowers in a warm preservative solution. Short stems may have to be placed in vials.

**Temperature.** Refrigerate gloriosa at 34° to 36°F (1° to 2°C) at high humidity.

## Consumer care

Recut stems and place flowers in water containing a floral preservative. Keep away from temperature extremes and out of drafts.

**ADDITIONAL READING**
Holstead, K.L. 1985. Exotics: handle with care. *Florists' Review* October 10:16-20.

# *Gypsophila paniculata*

jip-*sof*-i-la
pa-nik-ew-*lah*-ta

Family Name: **Caryophyllaceae**
Common Name: **Baby's Breath**

**Perennials with numerous small white or pink flowers in large, delicate clusters. Native to Europe and Asia; naturalized in North America.**

GYPSOPHILA

## Production factors

**Problems.** Browning of open flowers sometimes occurs, especially in warm weather. Overmaturation during long days at summer temperatures is suspected to be the cause. Botrytis may also be a factor. If flower browning is a problem, harvest baby's breath in the tight bud stage with little or no petal color showing.

## Postproduction factors

**Development at harvest.** Stage of maturity depends upon whether flowers are intended as fresh cut or dried flowers. For the remote fresh flower market, baby's breath is usually harvested with 20% to 30% of the flowers open. For the dried flower market, as well as for the local fresh market, baby's breath is harvested with 50% to 60% of the flowers open. In some instances, baby's breath is harvested at the tight bud stage with only 5% open flowers.

**Lasting qualities.** Fresh baby's breath lasts about 5 to 7 days in water, though somewhat longer in a preservative.

**Preservative.** Use a floral preservative to promote bud opening and extend vase life. Flowers in a preservative often last longer than those left intact on plants. Shipping baby's breath in containers of preservative solution enhances vase life. Overnight pulsing in 10% sugar and 25 ppm silver nitrate prior to shipping also increases vase life.

**Hydration.** Use clean, preferably deionized, water adjusted to pH 3.5.

**Ethylene.** Flowers are sensitive to ethylene and, when exposed, fail to open. Pulse baby's breath for 30 minutes in a silver thiosulfate solution (4 oz per gallon [120 ml per 4 l]) combined with 1.5% sucrose.

**Storage.** Properly hydrated baby's breath with about 50% open flowers held in a preservative solution may be stored for up to 3 weeks at 35°F (2°C). Generally, however, such long-term storage is not recommended. Don't store baby's breath dry. Flowers dehydrate easily, and buds fail to open.

G

# Gypsophila paniculata

## Retail handling

**Preparation.** Prepare fresh, open baby's breath for hydration as soon as possible to prevent wilting. Unpack flowers and recut stems before placing in solution.

**Pretreatment.** If flowers have not already been pretreated, pulse with silver thiosulfate for several hours at room temperature to reduce the effects of ethylene sensitivity.

**Preservative.** Use the same preservative for holding flowers as is used for opening buds.

**Temperature.** Refrigerate open baby's breath at 35° to 40°F (2° to 5°C).

**Bud opening.** Bud cut baby's breath with only about 5% open flowers may be opened in a preservative solution. Commercial preservatives are good, but a custom-made preservative may also be used with great success.

Various germicides have been used successfully in opening solutions. Among these are 200 ppm 8-hydroxyquinoline citrate with 100 ppm sodium benzoate or 25 ppm silver nitrate. The silver nitrate is said to be less phytotoxic and to produce whiter opened flowers. Add 5% to 10% sugar to the silver nitrate solution as an energy source. Another solution that improves bud opening of baby's breath is a 24- to 72-hour pulse in 300 ppm 8-hydroxyquinoline citrate and 10% sucrose. This solution is reported to be more effective than pulsing with 25 ppm silver nitrate and 10% sucrose.

Keep flowers at about 70°F (21°C) and 50% relative humidity in about 100 fc (1 klux) of light. Buds should open in 2 or 3 days. Refrigerate flowers when desired stage develops.

**Drying.** At least 50% of the flowers should be open before drying. Use the same solution recommended for opening fresh market bud cut baby's breath, 25 ppm silver nitrate and sugar, to open flowers for drying. To dry baby's breath, place stems in a solution of 1 part glycerine and 2 parts water. After uptake, hang bunches upside down in a warm, ventilated area.

## Consumer care

Recut stems and remove excess lower foliage. Place flowers in clean, warm water that has a preservative added. Keep baby's breath away from ripening fruit. Avoid high temperatures and rapid air movement.

ADDITIONAL READING

Anon. 1980. *Retail Florist's Concise Guide to Care and Handling.* Alexandria, VA: Society of American Florists.

Apelbaum, A. and M. Katachansky. 1977. Improving quality and prolonging vase life of bud cut flowers by pretreatment with thiabendazole. *Journal of the American Society of Horticultural Scientists* 102:623-625.

Besemer, S.T. 1983. Gypsophila flower browning. *San Diego Extension Notice.* San Diego.

Holstead, C.L. 1984. Fighting ethylene: positive prospects for the future. *Florist's Review* February 2 175(4496):32-36.

Jacquemont, R. 1985. Conservation solutions and quality in the French cut flower sector. *Comptes Rendus des Seances del'Academie d'Agriculture de France* 71(11):1219-1223.

Reid, M.S. 1986. "Postharvest care and handling of cut flowers." Department of Environmental Horticulture, University of California at Davis. April 15, draft version.

Sullivan, G.H., J.L. Robertson and G.L. Staby. 1980. Postharvest care and handling of fresh flowers and greens. Chapter 21. *Management for Retail Florists with Applications to Nurseries and Garden Centers.* San Francisco: W.H. Freeman and Company.

G

# *Heliconia* spp.

## hel-i-*cone*-ee-uh

Includes: *H. bihai, H. caribaea, H. psittacorum, H. rostrata*
Family Name: **Musaceae**
Common Names: **Heliconia, Lobster Claw, Wild Plantain**

**Bananalike foliage and flower stems from 1 to 6 feet (30 to 183 cm) with ornamental, often brightly colored, alternating boat-shaped bracts from 4 to 14 inches (11 to 36 cm) across encasing the true flowers. Native of the American tropics.**

SHARONII

## Postproduction factors

**Development at harvest.** Since heliconia flowers do not continue to develop after harvest, they must be cut at the stage at which they are to be used.

**Lasting qualities.** There are great differences in vase life performance among cultivars. Andromeda and Golden Torch vase life averages 14 to 17 days in deionized water at 75°F (25°C). Generally, the smaller the heliconia, the shorter the vase life, but even the smallest heliconias have a vase life of up to 7 days.

**Temperature.** Heliconias are very sensitive to chilling temperatures, even more so than bird-of-paradise. Keep at no less than 55° to 60°F (13° to 16°C) and high relative humidity.

**Shipping.** Heliconia must be packed and cushioned to prevent mechanical damage caused by shifting. Vase life is not affected by handling during shipping.

## Retail handling

**Preparation.** Unpack flowers immediately and recut stems.

**Hydration.** Place flowers in clean, warm water adjusted to pH 3.5.

**Preservative.** Use a preservative to retard bacterial growth in the water.

**Temperature.** Heliconias suffer chilling damage at temperatures normally used to store other flowers. Keep heliconias at or somewhat above 55° to 60°F (13° to 16°C).

**Storage.** Maintain high relative humidity during storage to enhance longevity.

# *Heliconia* spp.

## Consumer care

Recut stems and place flowers in a clean vase. Use warm, clean, preferably deionized, water containing a floral preservative.

**ADDITIONAL READING**

Akamine, E.K. 1976. Postharvest handling of tropical ornamental cut crops in Hawaii. *HortScience* 11(2):125-128.

Broschat, T.K., H.M. Donselman and A.A. Will. 1984. Golden Torch, an orange heliconia for cut flower use. *Circulars, Agricultural Experiment Stations* (S-308 and 309). Florida.

Broschat, T.K., H.M. Donselman and A.A. Will. 1984. Andromeda and Golden Torch heliconias. *HortScience* 19(5):736-737.

Elkilson, M.C. 1985. Heliconia flowers. *Flowers &* 6(11):63.

Holstead, K.L. 1985. Exotics: handle with care. *Florist's Review* October 10 176(4563):16-20.

H

# *Hippeastrum* hybrids

hip-ee-*as*-trum

## Family Name: **Amaryllidaceae**
## Common Name: **Amaryllis**

**Large-flowered, bulbous plant native to tropical Americas. The name amaryllis is generally used for hybrids of hippeastrum, the kind most commonly used as pot plants by florists. The true amaryllis, *Amaryllis belladonna,* is a similar plant grown as a field crop almost exclusively in California.**

H

APPLEBLOSSOM

## Postproduction factors

**Lasting qualities.** Amaryllis flowers last 10 days.

**Problems.** After flowers are placed in water, stem bases have a tendency to split and roll out; however, this does not affect keeping quality. Also, flowers bruise easily. Handle with care.

**Preservative.** Recut stems and place flowers in a warm—100° to 110°F (38° to 43°C)—preservative solution.

**Temperature.** Refrigerate flowers at 40° to 50°F (5° to 10°C). Within this range, stems can be stored dry to retard flowering.

Recut stems and place flowers in a preservative solution. Keep away from heat and drafts.

ADDITIONAL READING

Anon. 1986. Florist cut flower care guide. *Florist* March, 19(10).

Halevy, A.H. and A.M. Kofranek. 1984. Prevention of stem base splitting in cut *Hippeastrum* flowers. *HortScience* 19:113-114.

# *Iris* hybrids

Family Name: **Iridaceae**
Common Name: **Dutch Iris**

**Hybrids of bulbous perennials. Mostly blue, white and yellow in florists' iris. Originally native to the north temperate zones.**

IRIS

## Production factors

**Temperature.** Lower night temperatures during production are reported to yield flowers with greater longevity.

## Postproduction factors

**Development at harvest.** Irises are normally harvested at the "pencil" stage: a pencil of color projects beyond the sheaths. In winter months, all cultivars should be harvested with more color than in summer months.

The cultivar Professor Blaauw does not open readily when harvested at the usual commercial stage. To open properly in a solution it must be harvested when the edge of the petal is unfurled.

**Lasting qualities.** Irises have a relatively short vase life, lasting from 2 to 5 days, depending upon how they are treated.

**Preservative.** Use a floral preservative for significantly longer vase life.

**Hydration.** Use clean, warm water, deionized if possible, adjusted to pH 3.5.

**Ethylene.** Although irises show moderate sensitivity to ethylene (3 ppm for 1 day), causing forced unfolding of the bud and shorter vase life, the damage may not be great enough to recommend treatment with silver. Since ethylene inhibitors enhance longevity, however, further research is needed to determine whether treatment with silver thiosulfate is practical.

**Miscellaneous chemical effects.** Narcissus or daffodil stem exudate in the same container shortens the vase life of irises.

**Temperature.** Refrigerate hydrated irises at 35° to 40°F (2° to 5°C).

**Storage.** Irises may be stored dry at 32°F (0°C) for a few days. Or store flowers at 32°F (0°C) in a holding solution for 5 to 10 days. Higher storage temperatures reduce vase life. Flowers stored longer may fail to open.

## Retail handling

**Preparation.** Make sure bud tips are not curled or dried, as they will probably not

I

open. Recut stems and remove loose lower foliage.

**Hydration.** Place flowers in clean, warm, preferably deionized water adjusted to pH 3.5.

**Preservative.** Use a floral preservative to extend vase life.

**Temperature.** Refrigerate irises as close to 33° to 35°F (1° to 2°C) as possible.

**Miscellaneous chemical effects.** Do not arrange irises in the same container with daffodils or narcissus.

## Consumer care

Iris has a relatively short vase life. Recut stems and place flowers in clean, tepid water containing a floral preservative. Place irises in a cool location, and keep away from drafts, excessive heat, fruits, vegetables and wilting flowers.

**ADDITIONAL READING**

DeHertogh, A.A. and C.H. Williams. 1969. The handling of cut bulb flowers by wholesale florists. *Michigan Florist* 464:11,25.

DeHertogh, A.A. and G. Springer. 1977. Care and handling of spring bulb flowers and plants, Part 1; Suggestions on the use and marketing of bulb flowers and plants, Part 2. *Holland Flower Bulb Technical Services.* Hillegom, Holland: Netherlands Flower Bulb Institute.

Kosugi, K., M. Yokoi, A. Muto and N. Harada. 1976. The keeping quality of cut flowers as influenced by growth and storage temperatures. II. Dutch Iris. *Technical Bulletin No. 24 of the Faculty of Horticulture.* Chiba University, Japan.

Reid, M.S. 1986. "Postharvest care and handling of cut flowers." Department of Environmental Horticulture, University of California at Davis. April 15, draft version.

Sullivan, G.H., J.L. Robertson and G.L. Staby. 1980. Postharvest care and handling of fresh flowers and greens. Chapter 21. *Management for Retail Florists with Applications to Nurseries and Garden Centers.* San Francisco: W.H. Freeman and Company.

Systema, W. and L. Barendse. 1975. The keeping quality of cut flowers is receiving ever more attention. *Vakblad voor de Bloemisterij* 30(49):16.

Wang, C.Y. and J.E. Baker. 1979. Vase life of cut flowers treated with rhizobitoxine analogs, sodium benzoate and isopentenyl adenosine. *HortScience* 14(1):59-60.

Woltering, W.J. and H. Harkema. 1981. *Vakblad voor de Bloemisterij* 36(13):36-38.

I

# *Lathyrus odoratus*   *la*-thi-rus  o-doh-*rah*-tus

**Family Name: Fabaceae (formerly Leguminosae)**
**Common Name: Sweet Pea**

**Climbing annuals with tendrils and very fragrant, usually short-lived flowers. Native to Italy.**

BOUQUET MIX

## Postproduction factors

**Development at harvest.** In the past sweet peas were harvested when the last bud on the inflorescence was half open. Modern handling techniques have made it possible to harvest inflorescences with the first flower developed and just showing color and the rest at a less mature stage.

**Lasting qualities.** Flowers in plain water have a short life—a maximum of 3 days—ending with abrupt petal abscission. Flowers treated with silver thiosulfate and a floral preservative last at least 7 days or more.

**Preservative.** Sweet peas respond very favorably to floral preservatives. Uptake of sugar is essential for maximum vase life. The preservative should also contain a biocide. Use 8-hydroxyquinoline citrate at 300 ppm, as it is less phytotoxic than Physan 20, which reduces longevity and damages petals.

**Hydration.** Use deionized water to hydrate sweet peas.

**Ethylene.** Sweet peas are very sensitive to ethylene, which causes petal drop. Pulse flowers with silver thiosulfate to prevent early abscission and to promote development and opening of tight buds. Hold stems for 10 minutes in a silver thiosulfate solution (4 oz per gallon of water [120 ml per 4 l]). Rinse stems, then hold in a 4% sucrose solution at 70°F (20°C) overnight. (Prolonged pulsing may cause phytotoxicity).

**Storage.** Flowers that are pulsed with silver thiosulfate and treated with a preservative can be stored dry for 4 days at 35°F (2°C). Flowers hydrated upon removal from storage show little reduction in vase life. Prolonged cool storage does, however, reduce fragrance.

L

# Lathyrus odoratus    la-thi-rus  o-doh-rah-tus

## Retail handling

**Preparation.** Recut sweet pea stems immediately upon receipt.

**Pretreatment.** Pulse flowers in a tepid solution of 4 millimolar silver thiosulfate for 4 to 8 minutes at 70°F (21°C) to prevent petal drop caused by ethylene, to increase vase life and to promote bud opening.

**Hydration.** Use clean, warm, preferably deionized, water adjusted to pH 3.5.

**Preservative.** After pulsing in silver thiosulfate, place flowers in a preservative solution (or 4% sucrose plus 300 ppm 8-hydroxyquinoline citrate) for about 18 hours (overnight) in an ambient temperature of approximately 72°F (22°C) in an artificially illuminated area (cool white fluorescent lamps do nicely). After uptake of preservative, recut stems and hydrate sweet peas.

**Temperature.** Refrigerate sweet peas at 35°F (2°C).

**Bud opening.** Open bud cut sweet peas by placing in water after pulsing in silver thiosulfate and holding for 18 hours in preservative.

## Consumer care

Recut stems and place flowers in fresh, warm, preferably deionized, water in a clean container. Add a floral preservative, and place sweet peas in a cool location out of drafts. Keep flowers away from ripening fruit.

**ADDITIONAL READING**

Mor, Y., M.S. Reid and A.M. Kofranek. 1984. Pulse treatments with silver thiosulfate and sucrose improve the vase life of sweet peas. *Journal of the American Society of Horticultural Scientists* 109:866-868.

Nowak, J. and R.M. Rudnicki. 1975. The effect of Proflovit-72 on the extension of vase life of cut flowers. *Prace Instytutu Sadownictwa w Skierniewicach B* 1:173-179.

L

# *Liatris* spp.

lee-*aht*-ris

Mostly *Liatris spicata;* also *L. pycnostachya.*
Family Name: **Asteraceae (formerly Compositae)**
Common Names: **Liatris, Gayfeather, Blazing Star, Button Snakeroot**

**Tuberous-rooted, herbaceous, perennial plants with pink purple or sometimes white flowers on slender spikes that open from the top downward. Flattened, fasciated stems are not uncommon. Native to North America.**

FLORISTAN VIOLET

## Postproduction factors

**Development at harvest.** For best longevity in plain water, harvest liatris when at least one-half of the upper flowers are open. Flowers harvested in the bud stage will develop in a floral preservative solution.

**Preservative.** Use a floral preservative to dramatically increase vase life.

**Hydration.** Remove lower foliage and hydrate flowers in clean, warm water adjusted to pH 3.5.

**Storage.** Vase life is decreased by wet or dry storage at 40°F (5°C), but the use of preservatives significantly improves the longevity of stored flowers.

**Shipping.** Liatris has high resistance to damage and shows very little loss in longevity under normal shipping and handling conditions.

## Retail handling

**Preparation.** Recut stems and remove all foliage below the solution level before hydrating liatris.

**Hydration.** Following preservative treatment, transfer flowers to plain water.

**Preservative.** Pulse liatris for 24 to 72 hours in an ambient temperature of 70°F (21°C) with a solution containing 200 ppm 8-hydroxyquinoline citrate and 5% sucrose.

L

# *Liatris* spp.

lee-*aht*-ris

## Consumer care

Recut stems and remove lower foliage. Place flowers in clean, warm water containing a floral preservative.

ADDITIONAL READING

Apelbaum, A. and M. Katchansky. 1977. Improving quality and prolonging vase life of bud cut flowers by pretreatment with thiabendazole. *Journal of the American Society of Horticultural Scientists* 102:623-625.

Bakker, J. 1979. Which minor bulb crops react favorably to cut flower vase life preservatives? *Bloembollencultuur* 89(31):804-805.

Borochov, A. and V. Keren-Paz. 1984. Bud opening of cut liatris flowers. *Scientia Hort* 23(1):85-89.

Jacquemont, R.R. 1985. Conservation solutions and quality in the French cut flower sector. *Comptes Rendus des Seances de l'Academie d'Agriculture de France* 71(11):1219-1223.

Salac, S.S. and J.B. Fitzgerald. 1984. Influence of storage conditions and floral preservatives on *Liatris pycnostachya* cut flowers. *HortScience* 19(3):568.

L

# *Lilium* hybrids

*li*-lee-um

Family Name: **Liliaceae**
Common Name: **Oriental Lily (hybrids involving**
***L. auratum, L. speciosum* and others)**
Common Name: **Asiatic Hybrid Lily (cultivars such as**
**Enchantment and Connecticut King)**

**Herbaceous perennials with underground, scaly bulbs. Numerous forms and colors from hybridization. Native to the north temperate zones; many from Asia.**

ASIATIC HYBRID LILY

## Production factors

**Light.** Winter-cropped lilies grown without artificial light may be subject to bud drop.

## Postproduction factors

**Development at harvest.** Cut lilies are normally harvested when a few of the lower buds have begun to open slightly and show some color. They are easily shipped at this stage. Flowers may be harvested at a tighter bud stage, but opening takes longer, and some flowers do not develop well. Lilies harvested too tight result in poorer color, fewer opened flowers and often poorer quality flowers. Open lilies do not ship well, since open flowers are fragile and are likely to be damaged.

**Lasting qualities.** Cut lilies have a potential vase life of 7 to 14 days if treated with silver thiosulfate and a preservative.

**Problems.** Lily pollen may stain anything it touches. Remove mature anthers to prevent staining.

**Pretreatment.** Lilies are sensitive to ethylene and should be pulsed with silver thiosulfate for maximum vase life. Pretreatment, however, may cause some misshapen flowers. A 20-minute pulse in a silver

L

thiosulfate solution (4 oz per gallon [120 ml per 4 l] of water) provides longest life.

**Preservative.** Floral preservatives promote bud opening and increase longevity.

**Hydration.** Hydrate lilies in tepid, good quality, preferably deionized water adjusted to pH 3.5 for maximum uptake.

**Temperature.** Refrigerate lilies at 35° to 40°F (3° to 5°C).

**Storage.** Properly treated lilies may be stored for up to 4 weeks, but foliage may yellow or turn brown during even short periods of storage. Stored lilies that have been harvested too tight may not open properly. Botrytis can be a problem during storage.

## Retail handling

**Preparation.** Recut stems, remove lower foliage and pinch anthers from blooms.

**Hydration.** Hydrate lilies as soon as possible in warm, deionized water adjusted to pH 3.5. Do not allow flowers to become dehydrated.

**Pretreatment.** To increase vase life and promote bud opening, pulse lilies as soon as possible. Allow a 20-minute uptake of 4 millimolar silver thiosulfate, or a 2-hour uptake of the more dilute 1 millimolar silver thiosulfate, at room temperature. Or pulse flowers overnight (18 hours) refrigerated at 35° to 40°F (2° to 5°C) in 1 millimolar silver thiosulfate solution. Sugar may be added to the pulsing solution. The vase life of Enchantment lilies is dramatically improved by a 24-hour pulse in a solution of 1.6 millimolar silver thiosulfate and 10% sucrose, followed by transfer to water.

**Preservative.** After pulsing, transfer lilies to a solution containing a commercial floral preservative, or use 200 ppm 8-hydroxyquinoline citrate plus 3% sucrose as a holding solution.

**Problems.** Lily foliage generally ages more rapidly than the flowers. Where leaf yellowing presents a problem, follow the uptake of silver thiosulfate and sucrose with either a 24-hour pulse of 2,000 ppm $GA_3$ (gibberellic acid) or use 50 ppm of $GA_3$ in the vase water. This treatment also improves foliage quality of stored lilies.

**Ethylene.** Keep untreated flowers away from sources of ethylene. Lilies may be affected by their own ethylene emanations.

**Storage.** If fresh lilies are pulsed with 1.6 millimolar silver thiosulfate and 10% sucrose for 24 hours, they may be stored dry at 33°F (1°C) for up to 4 weeks without decreasing vase life. This method, however, can lead to some yellowing or browning, even after short storage periods. After pulsing with silver thiosulfate and sucrose, wrap flowers in polyethylene film to reduce water loss, and bring them to storage temperature as quickly as possible.

## Consumer care

Recut stems and remove lower foliage. Remove pollen-laden anthers to prevent staining. Place flowers in clean, tepid water to which a floral preservative has been added. Keep lilies away from ripening fruit.

L

**ADDITIONAL READING**

Boer, W.C. and R.A. Hilhorst. 1977. Shorter vase life for cut flowers after storage in a cool store. *Vakblad voor de Bloemisterij* 32(50/51):54-55.

Nowak, J. and K. Mynett. 1985. The effect of growth regulators on postharvest characteristics of cut *Lilium Prima inflorescences. Acta Hort* 167:109-116.

Nowak, J. and K. Mynett. 1985. The effect of sucrose, silver thiosulfate and 8-hydroxyquinoline citrate on the quality of Lilium inflorescences cut at the bud stage and stored at low temperature. *Scientia Hort* 25(3):299-302.

Reid, M.S. 1986. "Postharvest care and handling of cut flowers." Department of Environmental Horticulture, University of California at Davis. April 15, draft version.

Swart, W. 1979. The quality of the lily cv. Enchantment as a cut flower. *Bloembollencultuur* 89(34):902-903.

Systema, W., K.G. Elfering and A. Swart. 1984. Pretreatment improves quality and vase life of colored lilies.*Vakblad voor de Bloemisterij* 39(39):28-29.

Systema, W. and L.V.J. Barendse. 1975. Aspects of the keeping quality of cut lilies and freesias. *Vakblad voor de Bloemisterij* 30(48):12-13.

Woltering, E.J. and H. Harkema. 1981. *Bedrijfsontwikkeling* 12(2):193-196.

L

# *Limonium sinuatum*

li-*mo*-nee-um
sin-ew-*ah*-tum

Family Name: **Plumbaginaceae**
Common Names: **Notchleaf Statice, Statice;** *L. latifolium*—**Perennial Statice;** *Goniolimon tataricum*—**German Statice**

**Biennials treated as annuals with purple, lavender, rose, yellow, apricot or white flowers in clusters, suitable for drying. Native to the Mediterranean region.**

L

PETITE BOUQUET MIXED

## Postproduction factors

**Development at harvest.** Plants are normally harvested when most of the flowers are developed. Postharvest treatment with a growth regulator to promote bud opening allows harvesting at an earlier stage.

**Lasting qualities.** In solution statice lasts at least 1 to 2 weeks. Properly dried, it lasts about 1 year.

**Preservative.** Sugar is not required for bud development.

**Plant growth regulators.** Use $GA_3$ to promote bud opening.

**Storage.** Storage of statice at 36°F (2°C) for 4 days reduces bud opening and vase life, although growth regulator treatment is still effective.

## Retail handling

**Preparation.** Recut stems before hydration.

**Temperature.** Refrigerate statice at 40°F (5°C).

**Bud opening.** Place statice in a warm solution containing 0.1 millimolar gibberellic acid ($GA_3$) plus 30 ppm silver nitrate and hold at 70°F (21°C) in a lighted area until the desired proportion of open flowers is reached.

## Consumer care

Recut stems and place flowers in clean, tepid water. Use a floral preservative to help prevent fouling of vase water and stem rotting. To dry statice, open bunches and hang upside down in a well ventilated area until dry.

# *Limonium sinuatum*

li-*mo*-nee-um
sin-ew-*ah*-tum

**ADDITIONAL READING**

Anon. 1980. *Retail Florist's Concise Guide to Care and Handling.* Alexandria, VA: Society of American Florists.

Steinitz, B. and A. Cohen. 1982. Gibberellic acid promotes flower bud opening on detached flower stalks of statice (*Limonium sinuatum,* L.) *HortScience* 17:903-904.

L

# *Matthiola incana*　ma-tee-*o*-la　in-*kah*-na

Family Name: **Brassicaceae (formerly Cruciferae)**
Common Name: **Stock**

**Biennials with spiked inflorescences of single or double fragrant flowers in white and shades of purple, lavender, yellow and pink to red. Native to Europe.**

MIRACLE WHITE

## Postproduction factors

**Development at harvest.** Stock is generally harvested when one-half to two-thirds of the lower flowers are open.

**Preservative.** Although no research substantiates the effectiveness of floral preservatives with stock, use a biocide to control bacteria buildup in holding solution.

**Temperature.** Ideal temperature range for storing stock up to 3 days is 35° to 40°F (2° to 5°C). Flowers freeze at 30°F (-1°C).

**Storage.** Prolonged storage can result in loss of fragrance.

## Retail handling

**Preparation.** Treat stock as soon as possible to prevent water loss. Remove the woody base portion of the stem and any leaves that would be below the solution level.

**Hydration.** Use clean, deionized water at 80° to 100°F (27° to 38°C) to hydrate stock. Make sure containers have been scrubbed out, preferably with commercial bleach, and rinsed thoroughly.

**Preservative.** Use a floral preservative.

**Bacteria.** Use a biocide to prevent foul odor from developing in the vase water. Add about one-half ounce (15 ml) of 5.25% sodium hypochlorite (commercial bleach) to each 2 gallons (8 l) of solution. Test the addition of bleach on a small scale before using extensively.

# *Matthiola incana*  ma-tee-*o*-la  in-*kah*-na

**Temperature.** Refrigerate stock at 40°F (5°C).

## Consumer care

Recut stem bases, removing woody portions and excess foliage. Place stems in warm, clean water. Use a floral preservative to prevent odor in vase water.

Change solution regularly. Avoid excessive heat, drafts and direct sunlight.

ADDITIONAL READING

Anon. 1980. *Retail Florist's Concise Guide to Care and Handling*. Alexandria, VA: Society of American Florists.

Kofranek, A.M., H.C. Kohl and J. Kubota. 1975. Stabilized chlorine compound as a vase water additive. *Flower and Nursery Report* January/February: 5-7.

Staby, G.L., J.L. Robertson, D.C. Kiplinger and C.A. Conover. 1976. Proceedings of national conference on commodity handling. *Horticulture Series* No. 432: 46-47. Ohio Florists' Association.

Sullivan, G.H., J.L. Robertson and G.L. Staby. 1980. Postharvest care and handling of fresh flowers and greens. Chapter 21. *Management for Retail Florists with Applications to Nurseries and Garden Center*. San Francisco: W.H. Freeman and Company.

# Narcissus pseudonarcissus

nar-*sis*-us
soo-doe-nar-*sis*-us

### Family Name: **Amaryllidaceae**
### Common Name: **Daffodil**

Popular spring flowers with trumpet or crownlike corolla, in shades of yellow, white and orange. Many cultivars with bicolor flowers. There are some double forms. *N. pseudonarcissus,* the predominant narcissus cultivated for the florist trade and known by the name daffodil, is exemplified by the cultivar King Alfred.

UNSURPASSABLE

## Postproduction factors

**Development at harvest.** Daffodils are generally harvested when the flowers are starting to nod, referred to as the "gooseneck" stage. Flowers harvested at the fully open stage, however, have a longer vase life than those cut at the "gooseneck" or "pencil" stage. Since it is more difficult and less practical to ship open flowers, daffodils are typically cut at an earlier stage of development. Multi-flowered forms are usually harvested when one of the flowers on the scape is open and the rest are still in bud.

**Lasting qualities.** Flowers last 4 to 8 days.

**Pretreatment.** Tests indicate that ethylene may reduce the daffodil longevity. Use silver nitrate at 30 to 60 ppm, together with 3 to 7% sucrose to extend vase life from 4 to 6 days. Or use a regular floral preservative to achieve same longevity.

**Preservative.** Use a floral preservative at whatever stage of development at harvest. Daffodil's utilization of sugar differs from other flowers as evidenced by a change in ratios of various sugars in daffodil petals as the flower develops.

**Light.** Reports indicate that illumination during cold storage of bud cut flowers can result in intensified color when blooms open.

**Hydration.** Use clean, tepid water for maximum longevity.

# *Narcissus pseudonarcissus*

**Plant growth regulators.** Although the cytokinin 6-benzyladenine can extend daffodil vase life for a day or so, its use is not widely recommended.

**Bacteria.** Place daffodils in a solution of 1 millimolar sodium benzoate to increase vase life by 1 day.

**Storage.** Store daffodils dry and upright for up to 2 weeks at 33° to 35°F (1° to 2°C) and 90% relative humidity. Under these conditions, there is little loss in vase life.

**Miscellaneous chemical effects.** Do not place other flowers in the same container with daffodils, at least during hydration.

## Retail handling

**Preparation.** Unpack flowers immediately and recut stems.

**Hydration.** Use clean, tepid water.

**Preservative.** Use a commercial preservative at recommended concentration, or make up a solution of 200 ppm 8-hydroxyquinoline citrate plus 2% sugar.

**Temperature.** Refrigerate flowers at 40°F (5°C).

**Miscellaneous chemical effects.** Do not place other flowers in the same container with daffodils, at least while they are being hydrated, as slime exudate may reduce the longevity of other species.

## Consumer care

Daffodils have a short vase life even under the best conditions. Recut stems and place flowers in clean, tepid water containing a floral preservative. If possible, do not place other flowers in the same vase with daffodils.

ADDITIONAL READING

Almquist, T.B., M.A. Andrews and K.L. Gureber. 1984. Harvest and postharvest techniques of narcissus. *Minnesota State Florists' Bulletin* April 33(2).

Baarendse, L.V. 1974. Damage caused by Narcissus slime to various flower species. *Vakblad voor de Bloemisterij* 29(21):12-13.

Nichols, R. 1976. Box storage for several days does not affect vase life potential. *Grower* 85(20):1023.

Nichols, R. 1975. Senescence and sugar status of the cut flower. *Acta Hort* 41:21-30.

Piskornik, Z. and M. Piskornik. 1980. Effect of preservative solutions on the vase life of cut daffodils. *Zeszyty Naukowe Akademii Rolniczej im. H. Kollataja w Krakowie, Ogrodnictwo* 7(No. 158):17-32.

Reid, M.S. 1986. "Postharvest care and handling of cut flowers." Department of Environmental Horticulture, University of California at Davis. April 15, draft version.

van Beek, G. 1984. The influence of temperature during marketing on the quality of cut flowers. *Vakblad voor de Bloemisterij* 39(11):35.

Wang, C.Y. and J.E. Baker. 1979. Vase life of cut flowers treated with rhizobitoxine analogs, sodium benzoate and isopentenyl adenosine. *HortScience* 14(1):59-60.

N

# *Nerine* spp. and hybrids

ne-*reen*

Includes: ***Nerine bowdenii, N. flexuosa*** and ***N. sarniensis***
Family Name: **Amaryllidaceae**
Common Names: **Nerine, Guernsey Lily, Spider Lily**

**Bulbous plants with flowers in striking colors. *N. bowdenii* is electric pink; other species and hybrids are white and near red. Native to South Africa.**

NERINE

reports of silver thiosulfate treatment.

**Temperature.** Hold flowers at 45° to 50°F (7° to 10°C).

## Retail handling

**Preparation.** Unpack flowers immediately and recut stems.

**Hydration.** Use clean, tepid water.

**Preservative.** Test nerine with a floral preservative to determine whether its use is warranted.

**Temperature.** Refrigerate nerine at 45° to 50°F (7° to 10°C).

## Consumer care

Recut stems and place flowers in a warm floral preservative solution made with clean water. Keep in a cool location.

## Postproduction factors

**Development at harvest.** The flower stalk is harvested without leaves. Cut nerine when the oldest bud is mature and partially to fully open. Research indicates that bud cut nerines can develop in solutions. Flowers cut at the very tight bud stage may develop crooked stems.

**Lasting qualities.** Vase life differs among cultivars. In plain water, flowers last 10 to 14 days.

**Ethylene.** Nerine longevity is affected by exposure to ethylene, but there are no

**ADDITIONAL READING**

Funnell, K.A. 1984. Selecting the best time for bud harvesting nerines. *Commercial Horticulture* August: 31-33.

Holstead, K.L. 1985. Exotics: handle with care. *Florists' Review* October 10: 16-17, 20-21.

Nijlunsing, W. and L. Barendse. 1976. Packing and transport of *Nerine bowdenii. Vakblad voor de Bloemisterij* 31(4):19.

Woltering, E.J. and H. Harkema. 1981. Ethylene damage to cut flowers. *Bedrijfsontwikkeling* 12(2):193-196.

# *Paeonia* hybrids

pee-*o*-nee-a

## Family Name: **Ranunculaceae**
## Common Name: **Peony**

**Herbaceous plants with large, showy flowers in white, pink, rose and rose-red. Origin is primarily Asian.**

PEONY

### Postproduction factors

**Development at harvest.** If harvested when the calyx is tight with little petal color showing, peonies may not open properly. Flowers cut at this stage have a shorter vase life. For optimum storage and minimal damage in handling and shipping, harvest flowers when the calyx is loose and petals are showing true color or else with one petal unfurled. For immediate, local use, harvest flowers in the partially open stage.

**Lasting qualities.** If picked at the earliest stages, peonies last 2 to 7 days with or without preservative when held at 70°F (21°C), depending upon cultivar.

**Preservative.** Use a floral preservative to reduce opening time and increase vase life.

**Storage.** Buds harvested in the loose calyx stage can be stored dry, in darkness, in plastic-lined boxes at 32°F (0°C) for up to 4 weeks with satisfactory vase life. Storage may decrease longevity of the cultivar Mons Jules Elie. Storage may result in premature wilting in cultivars Felix Crousse and John C. Lee.

### Retail handling

**Preparation.** Recut stems and remove lower foliage upon receipt or removal from storage.

**Hydration.** For best results in opening bud cut flowers and hydrating open flowers, use clean water adjusted to pH 3.5 with citric acid.

**Preservative.** After hydration, transfer flowers to a floral preservative solution. Hold bud cut flowers at 70°F (21°C) until open.

**Temperature.** Refrigerate open flowers at 35° to 40°F (2° to 5°C).

**Storage.** Store freshly harvested bud cut peonies, in the loose calyx stage, in a polyethylene-lined box at 32°F (0°C) for up to 4 weeks.

P

# *Paeonia* hybrids

## Consumer care

Recut stems and place in clean, warm water. Use a floral preservative according to directions.

**ADDITIONAL READING**

Heuser, C.W. and K.B. Evensen. 1986. Cut flower longevity of peony. *Journal of the American Society of Horticultural Scientists* 111(6):896-899.

Nikolova, N. 1972. Methods of prolonging the life of cut flowers. *Bulgarski Plodove, Zelenchutsi i Konservi* 9:7-9.

P

# *Protea* spp. and related genera    pro-*tee*-a

Family Name: **Proteaceae**
Common Name: **Protea**

Large, woody shrubs/trees that bear artichoke-like flowers with stiff, colorful bracts. Other members of the *Proteaceae* family with handling requirements similar to those of the genus *Protea* are: Leucospermum—commonly called pincushion, in sunburst shapes of yellow and orange and, occasionally, pink; Banksia—spikelike, cylindrical clusters having a popsicle shape; and Leucodendron—grown for both flowers and foliage. Smallest of the commercial types. Available in a wide variety of colors.

PINK ICE

## Production factors

**Soil.** Proteas require a well-drained, acid soil for best leaf color.

## Postproduction factors

**Development at harvest.** Harvest when fully open, but before bracts separate from flower head.

**Lasting qualities.** Protea lasts from 2 to 6 weeks, depending upon genus. Pincushions have the shortest vase life. Flowers dry well, particularly protea, banksia and leucodendron.

**Problems.** Leaf blackening, which varies in severity with varieties, occurs in cut proteas. Use a preservative to reduce blackening.

**Preservative.** Use a floral preservative to enhance vase life, reduce leaf blackening and allow for higher shipping temperatures.

**Hydration.** For fast hydration, use clean, warm water adjusted to pH 3.5.

**Storage.** Proteas will keep for 1 week, dry, at 35°F (2°).

## Retail handling

**Preparation.** Recut stems and remove any leaves that would be below solution level.

**Hydration.** Use clean, warm water. For optimum hydration, place flowers in a solution of citric acid with a pH of 3.0 to 3.5 for 2 to 3 hours.

**Preservative.** After hydration, transfer flowers to a fresh floral preservative solution.

P

# *Protea* spp. and related genera    pro-*tee*-a

**Temperature.** Refrigerate at 35° to 45°F (2° to 7°C). Lower temperatures may cause injury.

## Consumer care

Recut stems and remove lower foliage. Place flowers in a tepid, freshly-made preservative solution.

ADDITIONAL READING

Akamine, E.K. 1976. Postharvest handling of tropical ornamental cut crops in Hawaii. *HortScience* 11(2):125-128.

Anon. 1986. Florist cut flower care guide. *Florist* March 19(10).

Paull, R., T. Goo, R.A. Criley and P.E. Paarvin. 1981. Leaf blackening in cut *Protea eximea:* Importance of water relations. *ActaHort* 113:159-166.

Porterfield, F. 1983. Contemporary design. *Florists' Review* 173(4489):26-29.

Seiden, A. 1983. Protea: care tips for florists. *Flowers & 4(7):47.

P

# *Rosa* hybrids

*ro*-sa

Family Name: **Rosaceae**
Common Name: **Rose**

**A large number of widely grown, deciduous, shrubby species. Complex hybridization of this popular flower has led to many colors, flower sizes and forms. Distributed throughout the Northern Hemisphere and in some cooler portions of the tropics.**

CORAL DESTINY

## Production factors

**Temperature.** It is reported that reducing the growing temperature to 55° to 60°F (13° to 16°C) during the last 3 weeks before harvest causes a definite reduction in vase life. Growing temperatures of 70° to 75°F (21° to 24°C) produced the longest vase life for cultivars Garnette, Zorina and Bacarra in tests. Higher temperatures reduce color intensity and postharvest longevity.

**Nutrition.** High or low levels of nitrogen and/or potassium, within reasonable limits, don't have a significant effect on vase life; however, soft growth and large leaves may reduce longevity.

**$CO_2$ enrichment.** $CO_2$ enrichment is not reported to influence vase life; however, soft, luxuriant growth and large leaves may result in a decrease in longevity.

**Disorders.** Powdery mildew, Botrytis and insect injury also reduce longevity. Ethylene produced as a result of infection may result in production of ethylene by the flower and improper flower development.

**Supplemental lighting.** Use of HID lighting for 24 hours produces soft, vigorous growth that results in excessive transpiration when harvested flowers are placed in water. If the water contains a floral preservative, rapid uptake of sugar often results in burning of the interveinal areas of leaves, followed by total leaf burn.

## Postproduction factors

**Development at harvest.** Proper stage of development at harvest depends upon variety and storage or shipping intentions. Roses to be shipped long distances must be cut at a tighter stage, which may result in variations in performance as cut flowers.

**Lasting qualities.** With proper handling, roses cut at the right stage of development can have a vase life of 6 to 16 days. Some consumers experience short vase life with

R

cut roses, and there are a number of reasons for this. The main causes are incomplete hydration and failure to maintain proper water balance in the tissues. These problems may, in turn, be related to poor water quality and/or failure to ensure adequate hydration prior to placing in a floral preservative. Other common causes of shortened vase life are incorrect use or omission of a preservative and prolonged or improper storage of flowers.

**Preparation.** Recut flower stems upon receipt if flowers have been out of solution for some time.

**Preservative.** Roses generally show excellent response to most floral preservatives, but actual performance depends upon specific water characteristics, such as clarity and alkalinity, as well as the relationship between preservative acidity, water alkalinity and the biocide pH optimum.

**Hydration.** Place roses in solution adjusted with citric acid to pH 3.0 for 30 to 60 minutes or until the foliage and petals become crisp and turgid. The amount of citric acid required to lower the pH to the desired level varies, depending on water source. The buffering action of salts in the water requires the use of greater quantities of citric acid to reach the desired acidity level, so test each water source to determine the correct amount of citric acid. In general, soft water has little buffering capacity, and a minimal amount of citric acid is required, while hard water has a large buffering capacity, and greater amounts of citric acid are needed to lower the pH.

**Ethylene.** Roses show slight sensitivity to ethylene, and research indicates that they respond to pretreatment with silver thiosulfate.

**Plant growth regulators.** Evidence indicates that senescence of roses is at least partially controlled by several plant hormones. The value of growth regulator supplements, however, has not been clearly demonstrated.

**Bacteria.** HQC is an effective biocide in rose preservatives.

**Temperature.** Although most florists hold flowers at above 40°F (5°C), the best temperature for roses is 32° to 35°F (0° to 2°C).

**Storage.** Roses may be held for 4 to 5 days at recommended temperatures in a preservative solution. Vase life may be reduced by longer periods in solution. To store roses dry, place them in polyethylene-lined cartons immediately after harvest and prechill to lower the temperature before sealing cartons. Store cartons of roses at 31°F (0°C). Upon unpacking, follow recommended procedures for hydrating. If flowers are dry or if they are to be stored vertically, hydrate prior to storage to prevent bent neck, which otherwise becomes permanent upon hydration.

**Miscellaneous chemical effects.** Leaf drop may occur if roses are placed in the same container with narcissus. Microbial populations associated with woody stemmed flowers (carnations, baby's breath) usually arranged with roses warrant the use of biocides in rose hydrating solutions.

## Retail handling

**Preparation.** Immediately upon receipt unpack roses, and remove lower leaves and thorns carefully, avoiding injury to the bark. Recut stems with a sharp knife or shears or in an underwater cutter.

R

**Hydration.** Place trimmed roses in warm water, 105° to 110°F (40° to 43°C), adjusted to pH 3.0 with citric acid for 30 to 60 minutes or until crisp. Then transfer to a floral preservative and move to a cooler.

**Preservative.** Commercial preservatives are very effective with roses. If a commercial preservative gives unsatisfactory results, test other brands to determine which is most effective in the available water supply. The best test is overall flower performance—size, color, crispness and longevity.

For retailers who wish to make their own rose preservative, the formulation below gives excellent results. In addition to the ingredients listed, a pH meter, litmus paper and a sensitive scale, all available from a scientific supply house, are necessary. Since precise measurement of very small ingredient amounts is required, making a preservative solution is cost efficient only if large quantities are needed (0.67 ounces per 5 gallons = 1 gram per liter).

*Citric acid*
Soft water: 0.06 ounces per 5 gallons (0.1 grams per liter)
Medium water: 0.2 ounces per 5 gallons (0.3 grams per liter)
Hard water: 0.45 ounces per 5 gallons (0.7 grams per liter)

*Sucrose*
Cane sugar: 13.4 ounces per 5 gallons (20 grams per liter)
Glucose/dextrose: 6.7 ounces per 5 gallons (10 grams per liter)

*HQC*: 0.04 to 0.67 ounces per 5 gallons (0.06 to 0.1 grams per liter)

*For soft water only:* Add KCl (0.15 ounces per 5 gallons; 0.225 grams per liter) and $K_2SO_4$ (0.17 ounces per 5 gallons; 0.261 grams per liter).

Add each of the ingredients in sequence to somewhat less than the final volume of water, mixing each one until fully dissolved. Then add water to bring to the desired volume. Test pH with a meter or litmus indicator paper. If pH is above 3.5, add very small amounts of citric acid and stir well, testing after each addition until pH 3.5 is obtained. Refrigerate solution until use.

**Floral foam.** Make sure roses are properly hydrated before placing in floral foam. Soak foam in floral preservative instead of plain water.

**Delivery.** Roses are best delivered in a preservative solution, but if they are to be delivered boxed without water, insert stems either in a small block of preservative-saturated foam or in vials containing preservative solution. If roses are to be delivered dry, make sure they have been properly hydrated and include a care sheet suggesting roses be placed in deep, warm, 105°F (40°C) water for 30 minutes before arranging in floral preservative.

## Consumer care

Remove lower foliage and thorns, being careful not to damage stems. Recut stem bases with a sharp knife or pruning shears. Place roses in clean, warm, 105° to 110°F (41° to 43°C), water containing a floral preservative. Avoid excessive heat or any other condition such as strong light or rapid air movement, which would cause rapid evaporation of water.

R

# *Rosa* hybrids

**ADDITIONAL READING**

Anon. 1980. *Retail Florist's Concise Guide to Care and Handling.* Alexandria, VA: Society of American Florists.

Durkin, D.J. 1982. Studies on the handling of cut rose flowers. Midterm Progress Report. *Roses Inc. Bulletin* May.

———. 1983. Hydration of cut rose flowers. *Roses Inc. Bulletin* April.

———. 1985. Studies on the handling of cut rose flowers. *Roses Inc. Bulletin* August.

Eisenberg, B.A. 1982. An evaluation of cut flower longevity in floral foams manufactured with and without a cut flower preservative. *Illinois State Florists' Bulletin* No. 404:6-7.

Halevy, A.H. and S. Mayak. 1975. Interrelationship of several phytohormones in the regulation of rose petal senescence. *ActaHort* 41:103-116.

Leeuwen, P. 1985. Pure water important for the vase life of roses. *Vakblad voor de Bloemisterij* 40(27):31.

Lemper, J. 1979. Roses after harvest. *Deutscher Gartenbau* 33(28):1179-1180.

Reid, M.S. 1986. "Postharvest care and handling of cut flowers." Department of Environmental Horticulture, University of California at Davis. April 15, draft version.

Staden, O.L. and W.H. Molenaar. 1975. The effect of different mains waters on the vase life of cut flowers. *Vakblad voor de Bloemisterij* 30(42):21.

Sullivan, G.H., J.L. Robertson and G.L. Staby. 1980. Postharvest care and handling of fresh flowers and greens. Chapter 21. *Management for Retail Florists with Applications to Nurseries and Garden Centers.* San Francisco: W.H. Freeman and Company.

**R**

# *Strelitzia reginae*

stre-*lits*-ee-a
ray-*geen*-ie

### Family Name: **Musaceae**
### Common Name: **Bird-of-Paradise**

**Exotic orange and dark blue member of the banana family. Several flowers in a sheathlike, pointed bract open sequentially. As one flower dies, a new one emerges, expanding the life of the inflorescence. Native to South Africa.**

BIRD-OF-PARADISE

## Postproduction factors

**Development at harvest.** Bird-of-paradise flowers are generally harvested when they are mature but have not yet emerged from the sheath. At this stage, the sheath shows a crack-like opening along the top and is somewhat swollen. Flower stems are often pulled from the clump rather than cut.

**Lasting qualities.** Properly handled, good quality flowers last 1 to 2 weeks.

**Disorders.** Botrytis can develop during storage as bird-of-paradise requires high humidity.

**Pretreatment.** Dip flowers in fungicide to discourage Botrytis.

**Preservative.** Longevity and opening of flowers is greatly improved by treatment with an acidified preservative. Pulse bird-of-paradise for 2 days with a preservative solution containing 10% sucrose, 250 ppm 8-HQC and 150 ppm citric acid.

**Temperature.** Store above 45°F (7°C) as bird-of-paradise are easily damaged by chilling.

**Storage.** Store *properly pretreated* bird-of-paradise in the tight bud stage up to 1 month at 45°F (7°C) and 85% to 90% relative humidity. Flowers harvested 4 to 5 days prior to the commercial cutting stage will open properly if handled in this manner. Chilling damage occurs in flowers stored for longer periods.

**Packing.** Because of their bulk, flowers should not be allowed to shift. Pack bird-of-paradise so they are firmly attached to the bottom of the shipping cartons.

## Retail handling

**Preparation.** Recut stem bases before hydrating.

S

**Preservative.** Pulse stored or unstored tight flowers in a preservative solution adjusted to pH 3.5 with citric acid for 24 hours. An excellent formulation for pulsing bird-of-paradise is 10% sucrose and 250 ppm HQC adjusted to pH 3.5 with citric acid.

**Special handling.** For immediate use of tight flowers, soak heads 20 minutes in lukewarm water, and make a one-half inch (1.3 cm) slit on the back of the pod near the stem. Reach in the pod with the thumb, gently lifting out the desired flowers. Then carefully pull the blossoms in a fan. Remove all older, senesced flowers before coaxing new ones from inflorescences held a few days.

**Temperature.** Avoid refrigeration if possible. Ideal holding temperature is about 45°F (7°C).

## Consumer care

Remove about 1 inch (3 cm) from the bottom of each stem using a sharp knife or pruning shears. Place flowers in clean, warm water containing a floral preservative. Remove flowers when they are withered to allow new flowers to emerge.

ADDITIONAL READING

Akamine, E.K. 1976. Postharvest handling of tropical ornamental cut crops in Hawaii. *HortScience* 11(2):125-128.

Anon. 1983. Bird of paradise: Care tips for the florist. *New York State Flower Industries Bulletin* No. 150, March.

Halevy, A.H., A.M. Kofranek and S.T. Besemer. 1978. Postharvest handling methods for bird of paradise flowers (*Strelitzia reginae* Ait.). *Journal of the American Society of Horticultural Scientists* 103(2):165-169.

Holstead, K.L. 1985. Exotics: handle with care. *Florists' Review* October 10, 176(4563):16-21.

Reid, M.S. 1986. "Postharvest care and handling of cut flowers." University of California at Davis. April 15, draft version.

S

# *Syringa vulgaris*

## si-*rin*-ga  vul-*gah*-ris

Family Name: **Oleaceae**
Common Name: **Lilac**

**Deciduous shrubs with flowers in white and shades of violet, bluish-violet and pink to red and burgundy. Native to Europe and Central Asia.**

BLUE SKIES

## Postproduction factors

**Development at harvest.** Harvest as flowers start to open.

**Lasting qualities.** Flowers last 7 to 10 days in water.

**Preparation.** The presence of foliage affects vase life. Remove all but uppermost foliage.

**Preservative.** Use a floral preservative to extend vase life to 8 to 14 days.

**Hydration.** Place flowers in clean, lukewarm water.

**Ethylene.** Lilacs are sensitive to ethylene.

**Temperature.** Store lilacs at 35° to 40°F (2° to 5°C).

## Retail handling

**Preparation.** Recut stem ends with a sharp knife or pruning shears. Never break stems. Remove all foliage *except that nearest the flower cluster*. Removing uppermost leaves reduces vase life.

**Hydration.** Place stems in clean, warm water adjusted to pH 3.5 with citric acid. Keep containers filled.

**Preservative.** Add a floral preservative to the holding solution.

**Ethylene.** Avoid exposure to ethylene sources.

**Temperature.** Store lilacs at 40° to 50°F (5° to 10°C).

**Problems.** Do not place freshly cut lilacs in water with other flowers.

## Consumer care

Recut stem ends using sharp pruning shears. Remove all leaves except those just below each flower cluster. Place stems in clean, warm water containing a floral preservative. Keep away from excessive

**S**

# Syringa vulgaris

si-*rin*-ga vul-*gah*-ris

heat and rapid air movement. Avoid placing lilacs near smoke, ripening fruit or other flowers.

**ADDITIONAL READING**

Anon. 1984. Increased demand for flowering shrub branches. *Holland Flower* No.13, December.

Eskilson, M.D. 1985. Spring flowering branches. *Flowers &* March.

Harkema, H. and E.J. Woltering. 1981. Ethylene damage to cut flowers and forced shrubs. *Vakblad voor de Bloemisterij* 36(22):40-42.

Zeller, C.C. 1986. Home is where the care continues. *Florist* March, 19(10):66-68.

S

# *Tulipa* hybrids

Family Name: **Liliaceae**
Common Name: **Tulip**

**Hardy, spring flowering bulbs with most stems terminating in a single flower. Single and double flowers of many colors. Origin is thought to be the Near East and Turkey.**

KEES NELIS

## Production factors

**Temperature.** Low nighttime forcing temperatures result in flowers with greater longevity.

**Forcing period.** Vase life correlates positively with the time of forcing.

## Postproduction factors

**Development at harvest.** Tulips are usually cut when half of the flower shows color, but the best stage of development at harvest varies with the cultivar. Cool flowers immediately at 35°F (2°C) in at least 85% relative humidity.

**Lasting qualities.** Many cultivars have a vase life of 5 to 6 days, though some varieties last only 3 to 4 days. Among the shorter-lived varieties are Apeldorn, General Eisenhower, Godoshnik, London, Oxford and President Kennedy.

**Preservative.** Preservatives tend to cause undesirable stretching of the stem, with only a minimal effect on vase life. Don't use preservatives with tulips.

**Hydration.** Water quality affects vase life. Use distilled or deionized water.

**Ethylene.** Exposure to ethylene inhibits stem elongation, but may reduce longevity.

**Storage.** Store flowers upright in water or dry in a horizontal position for short periods at about 35°F (2°C). Store flowers upright, dry, for up to 5 days. Wrap flowers tightly. Some cultivars may be stored for 2 to 3 weeks if harvested in the green bud stage with the bulb attached and held at 32°F (0°C).

## Retail handling

**Preparation.** Recut stem bases immediately prior to use.

**T**

**Hydration.** Place stems in 6 to 8 inches (15 to 20 cm) of tepid water. Keep flowers tightly wrapped to prevent permanent stem bending and hold at room temperature until flowers are turgid.

**Preservative.** Do not use a floral preservative.

**Temperature.** Refrigerate hydrated tulips at 35°F (2°C) for best longevity.

**Miscellaneous chemical effects.** The slime exudate from narcissus held in the same container drastically shortens the life of tulips. Don't place tulips with narcissus during hydration.

**Skin sensitivity.** Use caution—handling may cause skin rash on hands.

## Consumer care

Recut stem bases immediately and place tulips in clean, tepid water. Do not use a floral preservative as it may cause stem stretching. Keep tulips as cool as possible, away from anything that could cause rapid evaporation, such as heat vents, and check water level regularly. Tulips curve toward light, so place them in an evenly lit location. For longer vase life, avoid placing tulips in the same container with narcissus.

Note: Handling may cause skin rash on hands. Use care.

ADDITIONAL READING

DeHertogh, A. and G. Springer. 1977. Care and handling of spring bulb flowers and plants, Part 1; Suggestions on the use and marketing of bulb flowers and plants, Part 2. *Holland Flower Bulb Technical Services.* Hillegom, Holland: Netherlands Flower Bulb Institute.

Rasmussen, E. 1982. Reduction in the last internode elongation of cut tulips by ethephon. *Tidsskrift for Planteavl* 86(2):185-188.

Reid, M.S. 1986. "Postharvest care and handling of cut flowers." Department of Environmental Horticulture, University of California at Davis. April 15, draft version.

Sullivan G.H., J.L. Robertson and G.L. Staby. 1980. Postharvest care and handling of fresh flowers and greens. Chapter 21. *Management for Retail Florists with Applications to Nurseries and Garden Centers.* San Francisco: W.H. Freeman and Company.

Systema, W. and L. Baarendse. 1975. The keeping quality of cut flowers is receiving ever more attention. *Vakblad voor de Bloemisterij* 30(49):16.

van Eijk, J.P. and W. Eikelbloom. 1976. Possibilities of selection for keeping quality in tulip breeding. *Euphytica* 25(2):353-359.

Woltering, E.J. 1982. Extra feeding of cut tulips did not significantly improve longevity. *Vakblad voor de Bloemisterij* 37(6):43.

Yokoi, M., K. Kosugi and K. Shinoda. 1977. The keeping quality of cut flowers as affected by growth and storage temperatures. III. Tulips. *Technical Bulletin of the Faculty of Horticulture* 25:1-4. Chiba University, Japan.

T

# Zinnia elegans

*zin*-ee-a *el*-le-gahnz

Family Name: **Asteraceae (formerly Compositae)**
Common Name: **Zinnia**

**An annual available in numerous colors and forms. Native to the Americas.**

PULCINO MIX

## Production factors

**Development at harvest.** Harvest when flower is nearly fully open.

**Lasting qualities.** Zinnias last 6 to 10 days.

**Light.** Flowers produced in May or June under a natural photo period have a longer vase life than flowers produced February to April under a 14-hour incandescent photo period.

## Postproduction factors

**Preservative.** Use a floral preservative to increase longevity.

**Hydration.** Use deionized water to improve vase life.

**Ethylene.** Sugar in preservatives may cause ethylene production, resulting in damage to flowers.

## Retail handling

**Preparation.** Recut zinnia stems and remove foliage that would be below solution level.

**Hydration.** Place zinnias in clean, warm, preferably deionized water.

**Preservative.** Use a floral preservative to extend vase life.

**Temperature.** Zinnias keep best at 35° to 40°F (2° to 5°C).

## Consumer care

Recut stem ends and place in clean, warm water containing a floral preservative.

Z

# Zinnia elegans

*zin*-ee-a *el*-le-gahnz

**ADDITIONAL READING**

Mugge, A. 1983. Vase life and storage of annual flowers. *Gartenbau* 30(7):218-219.

Stimart, D.P. and D.J. Brown. 1982. Regulation of postharvest flower senescence in *Zinnia elegans,* Jacq. *Scientia Hort* 17(4):391-396.

Stimart, D.P., D.J. Brown and T. Solomos. 1983. Development of flowers and changes in carbon dioxide, ethylene and various sugars of cut *Zinnia elegans,* Jacq. *Journal of the American Society of Horticultural Scientists* 108(4):651-655.

Z

# FORMULATIONS FOR CUT FLOWER TREATMENTS

## Conversions

1 ounce= 28.3 grams
1 ppm = 133.5 ounces per gallon
1 kilogram = 1,000 grams = 35.3 ounces
1 pound = 16 ounces
1 gallon = 3.8 liters
1 liter = 0.26 gallons

## Biocides

**Hydroxyquinoline citrate (HQC) concentrate.** Add 3 ounces (90 ml) of HQC to 1 gallon (4 l) of water and mix thoroughly. This gives roughly 20,000 ppm. Dilute 1 to 100 to make a 200 ppm solution.

**Silver nitrate.** Use at 50 ppm (0.007 ounces per gallon of water or 50 mg per l).

**Household bleach.** Dilute 1 part bleach in 500 parts water in the final vase water. This mixture loses its effectiveness over time. Make fresh solution for each use.

## Hydration

Hydration refers to the uptake of water by cut flowers. Vase life generally benefits from good hydration which, in turn, depends on the degree of acidity or alkalinity of the water.

The term pH is a measure of acidity or alkalinity on a scale from 0 to 14. Seven is neutral. The further below 7.0, the more acidic the water; the further above 7.0, the more alkaline. Optimum water uptake in flowers occurs in somewhat acid conditions—about pH 3.0. Hydration is much slower at higher pH.

**Opening carnations.** To make a stock concentrate solution, dissolve 10 ounces (3 ml) of citric acid in 1 gallon (4 l) of water. Store stock solution in refrigerator. Add 1 ounce (30 ml) of concentrate to 1 gallon (4 l) of water. (For moderate conductivity water.)

**Standard hydrating.** Add 0.5 ounces (15 ml) of citric acid and 1 ounce (30 ml) commercial bleach to 8 gallons (30 l) of water.

**Fast hydration.** Add 0.3 ounces (9 ml) of citric acid and 0.2 ounces (6 ml) of HQC to 8 gallons (30 l) of water.

**Difficult cases.** Add 0.3 ounces (9 ml) of citric acid, 0.2 ounces (6 ml) HQC and 0.2 ounces (6 ml) of Tween 20 or Triton-X100 to 8 gallons (30 l) of water. *Keep flowers in this solution for no longer than 3 hours.*

Use a pH meter or litmus indicator paper *to determine the exact volume required to reach pH 3.5.* Use each solution only 1 day. Do not leave flowers in hydrating solutions with very low pH. After flowers become crisp and turgid, transfer to a normal preservative solution or water.

## Preservatives, long-term floral

Mix 0.38 ounces (11 ml) of citric acid, 0.25 ounces (8 ml) HQC (or HQS) and 20 ounces (560 g) table sugar in 10 gallons (38 l) of water. Adjust to pH 3.5.

*or*

Combine 0.2 ounces (11.4 ml) citric acid, 26.8 ounces (804 ml) sucrose (or 13.4 ounces [402 ml] dextrose or glucose), 0.3 ounces (10 ml) potassium chloride (KCl), 0.35 ounces (10.5 ml) potassium sulfate ($K_2SO_4$), and 0.03 ounces (1 ml) of HQC. Adjust to pH 3.5. This formulation is excellent for roses that have been hydrated in citric acid (pH 2.7 to 3.0) solution for 30 to 60 minutes.

## Silver thiosulfate

Application of silver thiosulfate (STS) renders flowers relatively insensitive to the effects of ethylene and is necessary to extend the longevity of carnations, snapdragons and other ethylene-sensitive species.

Mix a fresh batch of silver thiosulfate from a concentrate for each use.

**Concentrate.** Dissolve 5.5 ounces (156 grams) anhydrous sodium thiosulfate or 9 ounces (255 grams) prismatic sodium thiosulfate in 1 quart (0.6 l) of water in container No. 1. Dissolve 1.3 ounces (37 grams) silver nitrate in 1 quart (0.6 l) of water in container No. 2. Pour the silver nitrate solution into the sodium thiosulfate solution very slowly, stirring rapidly. *Lack of care during mixing will cause precipitation of the silver, and the resulting mixture will be useless.*

Add 0.64 fluid ounces (19 ml) of HQC biocide concentrate (see *Biocides* above) to the 2 quarts (2 l) of silver thiosulfate.

Use one of the following methods of applying STS:

**Short pulse.** Add 4 fluid ounces (120 ml) of STS concentrate to 1 gallon (4 l) of water. Pulse flowers 10 to 20 minutes at room temperature in this solution. Remove flowers, rinse stems and transfer to a preservative solution.

**Long pulse.** Add 1 fluid ounce (30 ml) of STS to 1 gallon (4 l) of water. Pulse flowers for 1 hour at room temperature, or overnight at 40° to 45°F (5° to 7°C).

STS **and sugar.** Mix 10% sugar together with 1 fluid ounce (30 ml) STS concentrate per gallon (4 l) of water. Pulse 1 hour at room temperature or overnight in a cooler. This treatment is effective with carnations.

**Special note:** STS is extremely toxic and must be disposed of carefully (in barrels to be processed). This material is banned in Europe and will probably be completely banned in the United States in the near future.

## Sugars, high concentration

Use 13.4 ounces (375 g) of sugar for each 1% sugar required in every 10 gallons (38 l) of solution. Table sugar (also known as sucrose or cane sugar), dextrose or liquid corn syrup may be used. Use somewhat lower proportions of dextrose or corn sweetener than sucrose to avoid burning certain flowers. Add the proper amount of sugar to a regular preservative to boost the sugar content. Most floral preservatives already contain between 1% and 2% sugar, so to attain a final pulsing concentration of 10% sugar, add between 8% and 9% additional sugar—or eight to nine times 13.4—which is from 107.2 to 120.6 ounces (3 to 3.4 mg) of sugar for each 10 gallons (38 ml) of preservative solution. Sugar concentrations ranging from 5 to 20% have been used successfully. Times for pulsing vary from 8 to 24 hours. Specific instructions are given for species that react favorably to short-term preservative pulsing in *Postproduction factors.*

# GLOSSARY

**Abscisic acid.** A plant growth regulator.

**AgNO₃.** See silver nitrate.

**Alar.** A growth retardant, n-dimethylamino succinamic acid.

**AOA (oxyaminoacetic acid).** Inhibits the synthesis of ethylene in plants. Not registered for postharvest. *May be carcinogenic.* USE CAUTION.

**Auxin.** A class of plant growth regulators.

**Biocide.** A germicidal substance that is toxic to certain organisms.

**Bleach.** About 5% sodium hypochlorite solution.

**Botrytis cineria.** A fungus, gray mold.

**Citric acid.** An acidifier used to lower a solution's pH.

**Cultivar.** A horticultural variety.

**Cytokinin.** A class of plant growth regulator.

**Deionized water.** Water from which salts and other ionic forms, such as acids and alkalis, have been removed.

**Dextrose.** A sugar.

**8-HQC .** 8-hydroxyquinoline citrate (oxine citrate). *May be carcinogenic.* USE CAUTION.

**8-HQS.** 8-hydroxyquinoline sulfate. *May be carcinogenic.* USE CAUTION.

**Ethylene.** An odorless, colorless gas that acts as a plant growth regulator.

**GA₃.** Gibberellic acid.

**Glucose.** A sugar.

**Hormone.** A plant growth regulator produced by the plant itself.

**Hydration.** Saturating the tissues with water.

**mM.** Millimolar; 1,000 mM = 1 molar; a 1-molar solution contains the gram molecular weight of a substance in 1 liter of solution.

**N-dimethylamino succinamic acid.** See Alar.

**NP.** N-1-naphthylphthalamic acid; not registered for postharvest.

**Oxine citrate.** See 8-HQC.

**Oxyaminoacetic acid.** See AOA.

**Parts per million (ppm).** Parts per million concentration.

**pH.** The measure of acidity or alkalinity, from 0 to 14; 7.0 being neutral, below 7.0 being acid and above 7.0 being alkaline; close to 0 is very acid; close to 14 is very alkaline.

**Phytotoxic.** Injurious to plant tissues.

**Plant growth regulator.** A substance that has an effect on plant growth or development.

**PPM.** Parts per million concentration.

**Preservative.** A combination of carbohydrate (usually a sugar) and a biocide.

**Pulse.** A short period of uptake, usually 10 minutes to 24 hours.

**RH.** Relative humidity.

**SDT.** Sodium dichloro-s-triazine. A biocide effective with chrysanthemum; *not registered for postharvest.*

**Silver nitrate (AgNO₃).** A biocide that also has the property of inhibiting ethylene action; immobile in the stem, it remains in the basal portion; disposal restrictions apply.

**Silver thiosulfate.** See STS.

**6-benzyl adenine.** A growth regulator in the class of cytokinins.

**Sodium benzoate.** A fixative available in photographic supply stores.

**Sodium dichloro-s-triazine.** See SDT.

**STS.** Silver thiosulfate. Inhibitor of ethylene action; usually used at a concentration of about 1 to 4 millimolar (mM). *Special note:* STS is extremely toxic and must be disposed of carefully (in barrels to be processed). This compound is banned in Europe and will probably be banned in the United States in the near future.

**Sucrose.** Cane sugar.

**Surfactant.** A substance that lowers the surface tension of water.

**Thiabendazole glycolate (TBZ).** A biocide effective with flowers such as gladioli, snapdragons and especially baby's breath; best used in combination with a sugar. *Highly toxic.* USE CAUTION.

**Tween 20.** A surfactant that lowers surface tension of water.

# CROP INDEX

# CROP INDEX